PGP & GPG

PGP & GPG
Email for the Practical Paranoid

by Michael W. Lucas

**no starch
press**

San Francisco

Printed on demand in the U.S.A.

ISBN-10: 1-59327-071-2
ISBN-13: 978-1-59327-071-1

Publisher: William Pollock
Managing Editor: Elizabeth Campbell
Associate Production Editor: Christina Samuell
Cover and Interior Design: Octopod Studios
Developmental Editor: William Pollock
Technical Reviewers: Henry Hertz Hobbit, J. Wren Hunt, Thomas Jones, Srijith Krishnan Nair, Len Sassaman, David Shaw, and Thomas Sjorgeren
Copyeditor: Nancy Sixsmith
Compositor: Riley Hoffman
Proofreader: Nancy Riddiough
Indexer: Nancy Guenther

For information on book distribution, translations, or bulk sales, please contact No Starch Press, Inc. directly:

No Starch Press, Inc.
245 8th Street, San Francisco, CA 94103
phone: 1.415.863.9900; fax: 1.415.863.9950; info@nostarch.com
www.nostarch.com

Library of Congress Cataloging-in-Publication Data

```
Lucas, Michael, 1967-
  PGP & GPG : email for the practical paranoid / Michael W. Lucas.-- 1st ed.
      p. cm.
  Includes index.
  ISBN 1-59327-071-2
  1. Electronic mail systems--Security measures. 2. PGP (Computer file) I. Title:
PGP and GPG. II. Title: Pretty good privacy & GnuPG. III. Title: Pretty good pri-
vacy & GNU Privacy Guard. IV. Title: Email for the practical paranoid. V. Title.
  TK5102.85.L83 2006
  004.692--dc22
                                                         2005028824
```

Liz:

-----BEGIN PGP MESSAGE-----
Version: GnuPG v1.4.0 (FreeBSD)

hQIOA9ooykGmcZmnEAf9Ed8ari4zo+6MZPLRMQO22AqbeNxuNsPKwvAeNGlDfDu7
iKYvFh3TtmBfeTKORrvtU+nsaOlbOi4PrLLHLYSBZMPauOBIKKGPcG9162mqun4T
6R/qgwN7rzO6hqLqS+2knwA/U7KbjRJdwSMlyhU+wrmQI7RZFGutL7SOD2vQToUy
sT3fuZX+qnhTdz3zA9DktIyjoz7q9N/MlicJa1SVhn42LR+DL2A7ruJXnNN2hi7g
XbTFx9GaNMaDP1kbiXhm+rVByMHf4LTmteS4bavhGCbvY/dc4QKssinbgTvxzTlt
7CsdclLwvG8N+kOZXl/EHRXEC8B7R5lOp4x9mCI7zgf/Y3yPI85ZLCq79sN4/BCZ
+Ycuz8YX14iLQD/hV2lGLwdkNzc3vQIvuBkwv6yq1zeKTVdgF/Yak6JqBnfVmH9q
8glbNZh3cpbuWk1xI4F/WDNqo8xOnOhsfiHtToICa2UvskqJWxDFhwTbbOUDiPbJ
PJ2fgeOWFodASLVLolraaC6H2eR+kOlrbhYAIPsxMhGbYa13xZOQVTOZ/KbVHBsP
h27GXlq6SMwV6I4P69zVcFGueWQ7/dTfI3P+GvGm5zduivlmA8cM3Scbb/zW3ZIO
4eSdyxL9NaEO3iBROFv9K8sKDttYDoZTsy6GQreFZPlcjfACn72s1Q6/QJmg8x1J
SdJRAaPtzpBPCE85pK1a3qTgGuqAfDOHSYY2SgOEO7Er3woXxGgWqtpZSDLEHDY+
9MMJOUEAhaOjqrBLiyPOcKmbqZHxJz1JbE1AcHw6A8FO5cwW
=zr4l
-----END PGP MESSAGE-----

BRIEF CONTENTS

CONTENTS IN DETAIL

2
UNDERSTANDING OPENPGP   27

3
INSTALLING PGP   39

4
INSTALLING GNUPG   53

5
THE WEB OF TRUST

6
PGP KEY MANAGEMENT

7
MANAGING GNUPG KEYS
99

8
OPENPGP AND EMAIL
115

9
PGP AND EMAIL

125

10
GNUPG AND EMAIL

137

11
OTHER OPENPGP CONSIDERATIONS

155

ACKNOWLEDGMENTS

Writing a book requires a lot of assistance from a lot of people. I am indebted to the following folks for their comments on various drafts and versions of *PGP & GPG*: Henry Hertz Hobbit, J. Wren Hunt, Thomas Jones, Srijith Krishnan Nair, David Shaw, and Thomas Sjorgeren. Stephan Somogyi at PGP Corporation also provided valuable insight into PGP and general encouragement. Len Sassaman also provided valuable insight into OpenPGP and its history, and reminders of how much the soft pillows of our expectations don't always match the airborne bricks of reality. What I've done well is due to these folks, while what I've messed up is my fault. Credit also belongs to the countless cryptographers, researchers, security administrators, and system maintainers of the world's OpenPGP infrastructure, not to mention Phil Zimmermann for creating PGP in the first place. Without them, I wouldn't have anything to write about.

Today's privacy debate is more intense than ever, and the mere existence of this book won't settle it. While David Brin might be right and the Transparent Society might be right around the corner, these days it seems that privacy is one-sided: big companies and government offices keep it, while us average folks don't. Hopefully, this book will give you the choice.

INTRODUCTION

Many people find encryption disturbing and even scary. After all, encryption techniques have been vital military and commercial secrets for millennia. Movies and novels use encryption as their plots demand, with total disregard for how encryption works in reality. Those curious about encryption quickly run headlong into formulas dense enough to repel anyone without an advanced mathematical background. All of this contributes to the air of mystery that surrounds encryption.

Doing the actual math behind modern encryption is admittedly quite difficult, but using the tools that do the work for you isn't difficult at all once you have a rudimentary understanding of when to use which sort of encryption. *PGP & GPG: Email for the Practical Paranoid* will take you step by step through the world of encryption and digital signatures and teach you how to use the tools that will allow you to protect your confidential information while sharing it as you desire.

This book is not meant to be the definitive tome on the subject. It will not teach you how to compute public encryption keys by hand, nor will it survey all the encryption algorithms and techniques available today. However, it will teach you enough about the ideas behind encryption and digital signatures that you'll be able to make intelligent choices about which of the available options you should use in any given circumstance. I'll demonstrate how to integrate encryption and digital signatures with popular email clients so that you can easily exchange secure email with others, how to install the Pretty Good Privacy (PGP) and the Gnu Privacy Guard (GnuPG, or GPG) encryption packages on Windows and Unix-like operating systems, and how to use them to secure your personal data.

NOTE *PGP is the original implementation of the OpenPGP standard, whereas GnuPG is a freely available reimplementation of that same standard. If the preceding sentence means absolutely nothing to you, you're starting in the right place. If you know exactly what that sentence means, you might want to skip to Chapter 1.*

The story of the OpenPGP standard begins years ago with PGP.

The Story of PGP

Encryption is an old science, and as computers became more and more powerful the number of people working with encryption grew and grew. Government officials grew increasingly concerned about the widespread availability of encryption techniques. Although encryption has perfectly valid uses for everyday citizens, it's also a powerful tool for criminals. In 1991, Senate Bill 266 (a sweeping anticrime bill) had a minor point that required government-accessible back doors in all encryption tools. While this bill was still under discussion, Phil Zimmermann combined some common encryption methods to produce the software he dubbed Pretty Good Privacy, or PGP. The ideas behind PGP had been known and understood by computer scientists and mathematicians for years, so the underlying concepts weren't truly innovative. Zimmermann's real innovation was in making these tools usable by anyone with a home computer. Even early versions of PGP gave people with standard DOS-based home computers access to military-grade encryption. While Senate Bill 266 was still threading its way through the legislative process, a friend of Zimmermann's distributed PGP as widely as possible in an effort to make military-grade encryption widely available before the law could take effect. The software was distributed to a variety of BBS systems as well as on the Internet (largely an academic and research network at the time, but still with worldwide reach). Their activism contributed to the demise of antiencryption legislation.

Zimmermann, a long-time antinuclear activist, believed that PGP would be of most use to dissidents, rebels, and others who faced serious risks as a consequence of their beliefs—in other words, to many people outside as well as inside the United States. Ever since World War II, the United States government has considered heavy-duty encryption a serious threat to national security and would not allow it to be exported from the United States. (For details, see the Wikipedia entry on "Export of Cryptography" at www.wikipedia.org.) Exporting encryption software, including PGP, required a license from the State Department, and certain countries could not receive such software exports under any circumstances. These rules were known as ITAR (for International Traffic in Arms Regulations) and classified encryption tools as weapons of war. Zimmermann decided to try to avoid the export restrictions by exploiting the difference between written words and software.

Zimmermann originally wrote PGP in boring old everyday text (or "source code"), just like that used in any book, and used computer-based tools to convert the human-readable text into machine-readable code. This is standard practice in the computer industry. The text is not software, just as the blueprints for a car are not a car. Both the text and the blueprints are necessary prerequisites for their respective final products, however. Zimmermann took the text and had it published in book form.

Books are not considered software, even when the book contains the "source code" instructions for a machine to make software. And books are not munitions;[1] although many books on cryptography did have export restrictions, Zimmermann could get an export permit for his book of source code. Thus, people all over the world were able to get the instructions to build their own PGP software. They promptly built the software from those instructions, and PGP quickly became a worldwide de facto standard for data encryption.

---

[1] Those of you who have dropped one of those big thick computer textbooks on your foot might take issue with this statement.

As you might guess, the US government considered this tactic merely a way to get around munitions export restrictions. Zimmermann and his supporters considered the book speech, as in "free speech," "First Amendment," and "do you really want to go there?" The government sued, and over the next three years Zimmermann and the administration went a few rounds in the courts.

This lawsuit turned Zimmermann into something of a hero in the computer community. Many people downloaded PGP just to see what all the fuss was about, and quite a few of them wound up using it. Zimmermann's legal defense fund spread news of the PGP lawsuit even further. In congressional hearings about encryption, Zimmermann read letters he had received from people in oppressive regimes and war-torn areas whose lives had been saved by PGP, contributing greatly to the public awareness of how valuable his work had been. Also, PGP was available on the Internet before the book was published—the code was available from anywhere in the world. (Admittedly, you needed Internet access to get a copy, which was slightly difficult in the early 1990s.) The book was simply a legal device to make it possible for people outside the United States to use PGP without breaking US law.

The story of the PGP lawsuit is fascinating and could fill a book this size or larger. Where exactly is the line between speech and computer code? Also, PGP was not distributed by Zimmermann himself, but by third parties. If someone in Libya downloaded PGP from an MIT server, was Zimmermann responsible? Lawyers fought these questions back and forth, but when it became obvious that the courts firmly believed that the First Amendment trumped State Department regulations, the State Department and subsequently the government dropped the suit. This not only saved them some time, money, effort, and humiliation at that moment but also prevented a legal precedent deeming encryption generally exportable. If a future administration desires, it can bring this issue back to the courts in more favorable circumstances against some other defendant.

OpenPGP

Even without the US government looming over it, PGP had some basic technical problems that cryptographers across the world quickly pointed out. The most glaring was that PGP made heavy use of the patent-protected RSA and IDEA encryption techniques; anyone who wanted to use PGP commercially needed to pay a license fee to the patent holders. Many computer scientists and security professionals found this unacceptable because they wanted an encryption system that would be freely usable by both the general public and businesses.

Zimmermann offered a solution in 1998, when his company, PGP Corporation, submitted an improved PGP design called OpenPGP to the Internet Engineering Task Force (IETF), the body responsible for Internet standards. OpenPGP defined standards by which different programs could communicate freely but securely by using an enhanced version of the PGP protocol and a variety of different encryption algorithms. This led the way for people and companies to create their own implementations of OpenPGP from scratch, tailoring them to meet their own requirements.

How Secure Is OpenPGP?

The OpenPGP standard is considered a military-grade, state-of-the-art security system. Although you see these words attached to all sorts of security products, OpenPGP is trusted by governments around the world, major industrial manufacturers, medical facilities, and the best computer security practitioners in the world.

That's not to say that OpenPGP is the be-all and end-all of computer security. Misuse of OpenPGP can reduce your security by making you believe that you're secure when you're not, much as if you leave for vacation and forget to lock the front door of your house. Poor computer-management practices might lock the front door but leave the key under the welcome mat for anyone to find.

Also, given sufficient computing power, it is possible to break the encryption used in any OpenPGP application. The National Security Agency (www.nsa.gov) is rumored to have computers specifically engineered from the ground up especially to break this sort of encryption. Of course, if someone is willing to spend millions of dollars to get your information, there are easier ways for them to get it, so I would say that when properly configured and used, OpenPGP is sufficiently strong enough to make people choose another method of violating your privacy rather than try to break the encryption.

Today's PGP Corporation

Today, PGP Corporation is a major player in the world of cryptography and information security, providing PGP software for many different platforms, from PCs to handhelds and even Blackberry phones. PGP Corporation software secures everything from email to instant messages to medical records.

PGP Corporation provides an implementation of OpenPGP that runs on popular operating systems. It provides a PGP system that integrates seamlessly with standard mail clients and desktops.

Although PGP Corporation was owned by Network Associates for a few years during the dot-com boom, it is now an independent company with a variety of big-name industry partners.

PGP is a commercial product, and PGP Corporation provides a whole range of related support services. We're going to cover the basic version: the PGP Desktop. (The corporate PGP solutions could fill a book on their own.) Because PGP is a typical commercial product, you are expected to pay for it.

What Is GnuPG?

GnuPG is a freely available implementation of the OpenPGP standard that was released to the public in 1999 by the German developer Werner Koch. It is available for both Windows and Unix-like computers (including Mac OS X).

Because GnuPG conforms to the OpenPGP standard, it can be used to communicate with people using any other OpenPGP-compliant software. "Freely available" means that you can get for free. You also get access to all the source code used to create the program, which is not directly useful to many readers but is vital to those who can do something with it. The formal name of the software is *GnuPG*, but many people simply refer to it as *GPG*. No matter which you use, people conversant with OpenPGP will understand what you're talking about.

WARNING *GnuPG is freely available, but that doesn't mean you can do anything you want with it. Any personal use is fine. Use within a company is also fine. If you want to use GnuPG within a commercial product and resell it, be absolutely certain to read the full General Public License (GPL) and comply with its terms! There is no such thing as "proprietary code" based on the GPL. You have been warned.*

PGP Versus GnuPG

Hmm. GnuPG is free, and PGP costs money. Why would you not always use GnuPG? There are several reasons why a person or organization might choose to purchase PGP rather than use the free GnuPG, or vice versa, including ease of use, support, transparency, and supported algorithms. All these reasons make the choice of encryption software very situation-dependent. Take a look at your options and pick the right tool for you.

Ease of Use

To use GnuPG, you must not be afraid to get code under your fingernails and tangle with the operating system's command line. Although various GnuPG add-ons provide a friendly user interface, they're not tightly integrated with the main product, and when the main GnuPG software is updated, these add-ons might or might not be updated. I wouldn't dream of setting up Grandpa with GnuPG unless I really liked talking to him five days a week.

PGP Corporation puts a lot of effort into making its products work transparently for the end user, in exactly the same manner as any other desktop program. As a support person, I find this extremely valuable. If I needed to set up the sales force, marketers, and accountants at my company with a single cryptographic solution, I would choose PGP in a heartbeat on this factor alone.[2]

Support

PGP Corporation has an extensive support organization. You can get phone support for the desktop products or have a whole team of consultants implement your company-wide PGP solution. When you buy PGP software, you get 30 days of free installation and setup support, which will allow enough time for most people to become comfortable with the tool. Support afterward exists at whatever level you require, for a fee.

GnuPG's support organization, on the other hand, is typical of free software. Users are expected to read the software instructions, check the GnuPG website, and search the mailing list archives and the Internet before contacting the mailing list for help. There is no phone number to call to speak to the "owner" of GnuPG. If you are the sort of person who wants to pick up a phone and yell at someone until they make your problem go away, GnuPG just isn't for you. Although you can easily find expertise in GnuPG and OpenPGP, and hiring a consultant to maintain GnuPG isn't that big a deal, that's very different from having direct access to the vendor.

Chances are that reading this book will give you everything you need to use either piece of software in your day-to-day communications. Although you might find an edge case for which one or the other program doesn't work, or you might discover a software bug, both programs have thousands and thousands of users who have exercised every piece of functionality countless times. If you have a problem, one of these users has almost certainly already had that same problem, asked for help on a mailing list or message board, and received assistance. I find that a web search answers questions on either tool far more quickly than a phone call ever could.

---

[2] The nontechnical staff at your company might be more tech-literate than mine. If so, you're more fortunate than you realize. Please tell me where to send my resume.

Transparency

Transparency refers to how much of the software is visible. For most users, this is irrelevant—they just want the software to work properly, without causing system crashes or scrambling their recipe collection. You're probably in this category. In the security industry, however, transparency is a vital question.

People who are serious about security—serious as in "billions and billions of dollars and/or many human lives depend on this information remaining private"—hire security experts to evaluate their security software and point out problems. The process of reviewing code and algorithms for problems is called *auditing*.

Encryption is an old science, and one of its primordial rules is that knowing how a good encryption scheme works doesn't help you break it. Encryption schemes that are available for review by the general public are the only ones that professional cryptographers take seriously. The cryptography behind OpenPGP has been continuously audited for 10 years now by people who would be delighted to find problems with it. Discovering a problem in OpenPGP would be a sure-fire way to gain fame within the cryptography community, much as discovering how to build a 100-mile-per-gallon, high-performance gasoline engine would be in the auto industry. Both seem impossible, but many people try.

However, both PGP and GnuPG are more than the algorithms used by OpenPGP. There's a whole bunch of source code in and around those algorithms. A bad guy could find a problem with that source code and use it to break the protection provided by the software. That source code requires auditing by skilled individuals to ensure its safety. GnuPG's source code is open for audit by anyone in the world and is checked by many different people of differing skill levels. PGP's source code is open for audit only to customers, but many of those customers hire very skilled people specifically to audit the code.

Algorithm Support

The original PGP used encryption methods that were encumbered by patents at the time PGP was created. Some of those encryption methods are now in the public domain, but one (IDEA) is protected by patents in Europe. OpenPGP has moved beyond all of these algorithms, but you might find references to them if you encounter old versions of PGP. You don't need to understand what IDEA is, but you do need to recognize it if you encounter it and have to deal with it.

GnuPG does not support IDEA because IDEA is less than completely free. IDEA is licensed under very liberal terms—it's free for non-commercial use; if you've ever bought a product that includes IDEA you have a lifetime, royalty-free IDEA license; and if all else fails you can buy an IDEA license online for $18.93. Those terms are modest, especially for modern software, but it doesn't meet GnuPG's standards. (Hey, it's their software; they set the standards.) You can hack GnuPG to support IDEA, but the GnuPG folks won't do it for you. PGP Corporation has paid the patent holder, and when you buy PGP you get access to that cipher. OpenPGP no longer requires IDEA, but some businesses might require it. If you find a 10-year-old encrypted file you need to open, you'll need IDEA. Otherwise, it's irrelevant.

OpenPGP and the Law

OpenPGP uses some of the strongest public-key encryption algorithms available to cryptographers anywhere. And I do mean *strong*. Law enforcement officials cannot break into a file properly protected with GnuPG, and some governments just don't like their citizens having such strong protection. Some countries allow their citizens to use strong encryption algorithms, but only in a limited and breakable manner. Others require that all encryption keys be given to a "key escrow" agency, so that if you become a criminal mastermind the government can get your key from the escrow agency and decrypt your incriminating messages. This is much like asking muggers to register their Saturday Night Specials before committing holdups—and roughly as effective.

To make matters more confusing, these laws change irregularly. If you are in doubt about the laws regarding encryption use in your country, check with a local computing professional or lawyer. Googling for "encryption law survey" will uncover several websites on the topic, including a very good survey at http://rechten.uvt.nl/koops/cryptolaw. (We discuss other legal implications of OpenPGP in Chapter 11.)

What This Book Contains

Although this isn't an exhaustive treatise on cryptography, we do cover a broad spectrum of OpenPGP, PGP, and GnuPG topics.

Chapter 1, "Cryptography Kindergarten," covers the basic ideas behind encryption. I discuss the basic encryption types used by OpenPGP, what separates an encryption system from a code, and when you should use each sort of encryption with GnuPG.

Chapter 2, "Understanding OpenPGP," teaches you the basic ideas underlying OpenPGP. I discuss the Web of Trust, keys and subkeys, keyrings, and keyservers, as well as ideas you must understand before installing either package. I also discuss how to safely handle your key, how to get your key signed or revoked, and how to make your key publicly available.

Chapter 3, "Installing PGP," guides you through installing the PGP desktop client.

Chapter 4, "Installing GnuPG," walks you through installing GnuPG on both Windows and Unix-like systems.

Chapter 5, "The Web of Trust," discusses how OpenPGP keys are connected to one another, identity verification, and keysigning. This is perhaps the most important part of Open-PGP usage, and is what makes the system unique. Real security doesn't come from software; it comes from people. Unfortunately, people are also the weakest part of any security system. Here I discuss both good and bad ways to handle keysigning.

Chapter 6, "PGP Key Management," takes you through managing the Web of Trust with PGP software.

Chapter 7, "Managing GnuPG Keys," shows you how to manage the Web of Trust with GnuPG.

Chapter 8, "OpenPGP and Email," discusses how to integrate OpenPGP into your email and some of the issues that can arise with email usage and PGP. We cover topics such as clearsigning versus PGP/MIME, retaining copies of encrypted messages, and so on.

Chapter 9, "PGP and Email," discusses how to use PGP software with email.

Chapter 10, "GnuPG and Email," covers integrating GnuPG with various email clients.

Chapter 11, "Other OpenPGP Considerations," shows you how to deal with some of the things that can go wrong with OpenPGP, how to use OpenPGP as part of a group of people, and how to use some other significant features in GnuPG and PGP.

Stop Wasting My Precious Time. What Do I Need to Read?

This book covers a single encryption system that happens to have two annoyingly different implementations. You need to read only the parts that apply to you, but which parts are those?

Carefully read the discussion of PGP and GnuPG earlier in this introduction and make your choice.

If you want to use PGP, read the chapters about general OpenPGP and those dedicated to PGP. That's Chapters 1–3, 5–6, 8–9, and 11.

If you choose GnuPG, read the general OpenPGP chapters and those dedicated to GnuPG: Chapters 1–2, 4–5, 7–8, and 11. GnuPG chapters tend to be longer than PGP chapters because GnuPG people must learn more.

Of course, if you want to master both sets of software, read the whole book! It's not that long, and some day you will be glad you did.

1

CRYPTOGRAPHY KINDERGARTEN

You don't need to understand everything about modern cryptography to use OpenPGP successfully. You do need to know some of the basics, however, and you must understand the protections that OpenPGP does and does not provide. This chapter provides a very brief and stripped-down introduction to the ideas behind modern cryptography.

What OpenPGP Can Do

Everything in the rest of this chapter builds to a description of the way OpenPGP works its magic. By combining hashes, public-key encryption, and digital signatures, OpenPGP allows you to achieve excellent levels of confidentiality, integrity, nonrepudiation, and authenticity. These terms have very specific meanings, which we'll discuss in this chapter. As an end user, you should understand how OpenPGP works so that you understand its limitations.

OpenPGP can do only six things, which are all missing from today's email architecture, and are extremely valuable in many circumstances. What you do with OpenPGP is determined by which of the six tasks you want to accomplish. Have a look at Table 1-1.

Table 1-1: Key Usages

Desired Effect	Action
I want anyone who reads this message to know beyond a doubt that I sent it—I cannot repudiate it.	Digitally sign the message with your private key.
I want to verify the identity of the person who sent a digitally signed message to see whether the apparent sender is the real sender.	Verify the signature with the sender's public key.
I want to send a message that only my intended recipient can read.	Encrypt the message with the recipient's public key.
I want to decrypt a message that I received.	Decrypt the message with your private key.
I want my message to be readable only by my intended recipient, and I want the recipient to be able to verify that the message came from me.	Encrypt the message with the recipient's public key and digitally sign the message with your private key.
I want to decrypt and verify a message that includes a digital signature.	Decrypt the message with your private key and verify the signature with the sender's public key.

When in doubt, consult this table! Although cryptography can be used in any number of ways, this table covers almost all common usages of OpenPGP.

Let's go on to see how OpenPGP accomplishes these tasks.

Terminology

Terms such as *code, cipher, cryptosystem, encryption system, encryption, encoding,* and so on have been flung around interchangeably for so long that most people think that they're all the same thing. Most people are wrong. You don't need to master the language of cryptography, but before we begin, we need to agree on the words we're using.

Plaintext and Ciphertext

Cryptography protects a *message*, or a piece of information. This message can be an email message, your company's financial records, a picture of your dog, or anything at all. In its original unencrypted form, this information is in *plaintext*, which is text that a person can look at and read without the use of any special software. (In the case of a spreadsheet or a digital photo, you need the proper software to view the plaintext, but it's usually viewable.)

After plaintext has been encrypted, a person looking at it sees the *ciphertext*. For example, if you look at an encrypted spreadsheet with your spreadsheet program, you'll see only ciphertext "garbage."

For example, here's a perfectly legitimate plaintext message that certain people would have been very happy to intercept a few decades ago:

```
Attack Pearl Harbor December 7
```

After you run this message through OpenPGP to change it to ciphertext, it changes just a little, as follows:

```
-----BEGIN ❶PGP MESSAGE-----
Version: ❷GnuPG v1.4.0 (❸FreeBSD)

hQEOA2HvKhYFm1VREAP/QlSUVjc89OHbalb6+MNceJdJjaVb2FGZGFSowg1IkCYr
b+wjMY4zOHoPty1hzW1wqPsWSiMLxZl24HQWWOPan8K2+LesErqeig4HEbMP23u4
QdUv4iOq9T1hoNvVboIypXluMIquze2r8r+X3hllwqAOn9ahz5VnVKj/OVnQi8OE
...
```

Good luck guessing what this means! Although a reader can easily see that this is ❶ an OpenPGP message encrypted with ❷ software and ❸ the operating system it originated on, that information won't be of much use to most eavesdroppers. The bad guys could use this information to get a hint about how to attack your computer, but that requires an entirely different skill set than attacking OpenPGP.

Codes

A *code* is a general term for any method of concealing the contents of a message. For example, some ancient military leaders would write a message on a strip of paper carefully wrapped around a stick, so that the message would be scrambled when the paper was unwrapped. Only someone who knew how to wind the paper and had a stick of the same size could read the message. This is a perfectly legitimate code and it was especially useful in an age when the written word was a mystery to most people. These days, however, it would be less-than-adequate protection against the prying eyes of anyone who has passed third grade.

Ciphers

One type of code is the *cipher*, which conceals the contents of a message by transforming each character in some way. One cipher that most kids play with at one time or another is a code that matches the letters in the alphabet to numbers ("A=1, B=2, C=3," and so on), with the text message then written as a series of numbers instead of letters.

This is, however, a poor cipher for serious use. Not only is it widely known, but a cryptographer who somehow managed to start a career without knowing this cipher could decrypt a medium-sized ciphertext just by counting how frequently the various numbers appear in the encrypted text and knowing how frequently letters appear in average plaintext.

Hashes

A *hash* is a specialized mathematical computation performed on a message, based on one of many algorithms. Related to a cipher, a hash is a very useful tool for OpenPGP. If the original message changes in any way, the hash of that message is completely different. For example, the message "Attack Pearl Harbor December 7" has the following hash (using the SHA1 algorithm):

e8e0ee9cdc6cd03c880b5870983bb02d48fceaea

Ugly looking thing, isn't it? Suppose that someone intercepted our message en route, edited it to read "Attack Pearl Harbor December 6," and sent it on its way. This one-character change would produce a completely different hash, like this:

07937cc5fd92504006f5f192d95cf8d341a26d18

A very minor change in the message creates a totally different hash! Although you might miss the change in the message, even the most cursory hash comparison would make anyone take notice.

You cannot recover plaintext from a hash. Also, constructing a file that would create a given hash value is very difficult; the fastest way to create just a file is to try all possible files. Given a hash, there is no shortcut to producing a file that matches that hash.

You'll also see references to checksums, which are error-checking algorithms similar to hashes but not as error-proof. Checksums are simpler to produce (and easier to falsify!) than hashes, but are useful for basic integrity checking.

Cryptanalysis

Attempting to decrypt a ciphertext without the key, by this or any other method, is called *cipher analysis, cryptanalysis,* or an *attack.* More complicated ciphers rearrange the letters in a particular manner or radically transform the plaintext so that it resists analysis by methods such as character counting.

Generally, ciphers combine the plaintext with a *key* to generate the ciphertext. The type of key depends on the *algorithm,* or the method used to combine the plaintext with the key. Similarly, you can recover the plaintext by combining the ciphertext with the key.

Goals of PGP's Cryptography

OpenPGP's cryptographic system has three fundamental features: confidentiality, integrity, and nonrepudiation (discussed in the following sections). These features combine to provide authenticity.

Confidentiality

Confidentiality means that the message contents remain private. The plaintext cannot be viewed by anyone who doesn't have the necessary keys, algorithms, and tools. In many cases, you cannot prevent someone from viewing the ciphertext, especially because every message that passes over the Internet can be viewed by a large number of people, just as letters left for the postman can be steamed open by a nosy neighbor. The ciphertext is incomprehensible gibberish to anyone who doesn't have the key to read it, however. Confidentiality is the first thing that comes to mind when most people think of a "secret code."

Integrity

Integrity refers to keeping a message unchanged. By using OpenPGP, you can confirm that a message has not been tampered with during transmission.

In many computer systems, such as those found in a typical office, the systems administrator has unlimited ability to not only view documents but also to edit them. Although most systems administrators are too ethical (and too interested in remaining employed) to transform their workplace into a real-life *The Young and the Restless* by carefully editing email, it is entirely possible for someone with even modest skills to do exactly that. Fortunately, the integrity provided by OpenPGP will notify the message recipient if a message has been tampered with, putting a stop to such shenanigans before they begin.

Nonrepudiation

Nonrepudiation means that a person cannot deny signing a particular message, which is especially important in the context of email.

For example, suppose that one day your boss receives an email that appears to be from you, containing your resignation in addition to threats to publish those "special" photographs you took of him and his pet goat if he doesn't offer you a severance package bigger than last year's corporate profits. You will probably want to say that the message is a fake. In other words, you want to *repudiate* the message.[1] If the message is not signed with an OpenPGP application, it will be very difficult to prove that you actually sent it; if it's signed with OpenPGP, however, you cannot repudiate it.

Nonrepudiation alone makes it worthwhile to use OpenPGP. If people know that email from you is habitually OpenPGP-signed, they will know that an unsigned message is probably faked, especially if its contents seem out of character. (It is possible that someone could have stolen your private key, but we'll discuss how to prevent that in Chapter 2 and throughout the book.)

This situation might seem extreme or contrived, but I have had to track down "forged" emails more than once. On only one occasion, the message was actually forged; more commonly, users send emails while highly emotional, intoxicated, or otherwise mentally incapacitated.

WARNING *Do not digitally sign email while drunk or emotional. Sending email at all in such a state is very inadvisable.*

Authenticity

Think about all these effects occurring simultaneously. When you receive an email that has been encrypted and signed with OpenPGP, you know that the contents of the message have

---

[1] Or not. If you actually have the goat pictures, it might be worth trying.

been concealed from any eavesdroppers. You know that the content of the message has not been changed. You also know that the message comes from a person who has the right to send such a message in the sender's name. This message is unquestionably *authentic*. The bad guys haven't gotten to you.

MALLORY: THE ORIGINAL BAD GUY

When you read OpenPGP (or any cryptographic) documentation for any length of time, you'll see references to someone named *Mallory*. Mallory is the example bad guy who wants to steal your information. The name Mallory is now applied to anyone who tries to break your encryption by any means. The name, which appears intermittently throughout the OpenPGP documentation, refers to any bad guy—not some specific person named Mallory. The Internet—indeed, the world—is full of Mallorys.

Encryption Algorithms

An *encryption algorithm* is a method for transforming ciphertext into plaintext and back again. Algorithms range from the simple (A=1) to the horrendously complicated. Some algorithms that are more resistant to cryptanalysis than others are called "better" or "stronger" than algorithms that a cryptographer can break more easily. Different algorithms have different sorts of keys.

A very common characteristic of computer-based codes is a *bit*, and the term often gets thrown around by people who don't know what they're doing. "This website uses 128-bit encryption, it must be secure!" "I'm using only 40-bit encryption, so I'm not really secure." The number of bits is just the number of ones and zeros in the key. A key with 40 ones and zeros is a 40-bit key. To guess a key, you must try every possible combination of ones and zeros. Because a 40-bit key has billions of possible values, guessing all possible keys would take a very long time. A 128-bit key has approximately 300 trillion trillion possible values, making guessing the key even more difficult. As computers get faster, the length of time to guess drops, but at this time it still exceeds a human lifetime.

Most cryptanalysis experts don't even try to guess the key. Instead, they attack the algorithm. If you have a 128-bit key, but your algorithm doesn't make good use of that key, it might be possible to either decode the ciphertext without the key or guess a large part of the key from the encrypted text. If your key is 40 bits, but you can guess 30 of those bits because of some weakness in the algorithm, the task of guessing the remaining 10 bits becomes much much easier. There are only 1024 possible combinations of 10 bits, and a computer can run through those combinations in very little time. The reality is that the security of a transaction is far more dependent on the algorithm used than on the number of bits used. Some algorithms are more secure with 80-bit keys than other algorithms with 160-bit keys because some algorithms are simply stronger than others.

You can think of algorithms and bits much like tires. A semi has 18 tires in motion simultaneously, whereas your car has only 4 tires. You car isn't any less useful than a semi, however—it's just used in different circumstances. Your car would not be improved by adding 14 more wheels (unless you're on one of those TV shows in which they do weird things to innocent vehicles, of course).

Algorithms have many different characteristics, most of which are completely irrelevant to a OpenPGP user. You do need to understand two basic types of algorithms, however: symmetric and asymmetric algorithms.

Symmetric Algorithms

A *symmetric algorithm* uses a single key for both encryption and decryption. The children's substitution cipher we discussed previously uses a very simple symmetric algorithm: Replace each letter by the number in the key. After you have this key, you can encrypt and decrypt messages to your heart's content. You can, of course, change the key easily: You and your correspondent could agree that "A=9, B=&," and then generate very different-looking ciphertext from the same messages. Although people could analyze your old messages and figure out your old key, they would have to start all over again after you change the key. When most people think of codes, they think of symmetric encryption.

The challenge with using symmetric algorithms is that you need a secure way to pass the key back and forth without it being intercepted. But then if you had that secure path, you probably wouldn't need the cipher in the first place! Despite appearances, if you're using the Internet, you don't have a secure path. The Internet is always tapped, and there are people who save every packet they receive on their network in case they become interesting later. I know of one network manager who has saved every packet that has crossed his Internet circuit in the last *five years*!

Asymmetric Algorithms

Symmetric algorithms are usually much easier to attack than *asymmetric algorithms*, which use different keys for encryption and decryption. You've probably seen old movies in which people cut a coin in a jigsaw pattern so two people who never met before know that they are speaking with the correct person. Asymmetric encryption keys work just like that: You must have both halves of the key to have unfettered access to the message. You encrypt the message with one unique key, and the recipient decrypts it with a different unique key. Although this process might seem miraculous to someone who has worked with only the basic substitution cipher, it does work. It doesn't matter which key is used for which action; if you use key A to encrypt a message, the recipient must use key B to decrypt it, but if someone encrypts the message with key B, only key A can decrypt it. (The math to show why this works is quite hairy, and the actual calculations are nearly impossible to perform by hand—they rely on the difficulty of working with extremely large prime numbers.)

When using asymmetric algorithms, two different people can carry around separate but matching keys and use them for private communication. It is practically impossible to decrypt a message given only one key, and having one key doesn't help an attacker figure out what the other key is. Asymmetric encryption became popular only with the spread of powerful computers that could handle the nightmarish math quickly and routinely. OpenPGP is based on asymmetric encryption.

DON'T MAKE YOUR BRAIN MELT!

Many people have a hard time accepting the idea of asymmetric encryption. They think that there can't be such a thing, that the idea is misstated, or (worst of all) that they *do* understand it. Googling for "asymmetric encryption" provides any number of papers on the topic. If you're truly interested and can handle the math, you're welcome to prove that it works. Bruce Schneier's *Applied Cryptography* is perhaps the most approachable work on the subject. Otherwise, don't let your ego interfere; just accept that numbers act really, really strangely when they get really, really big.

Having a single cryptographic key made up of keys A and B opens up an interesting possibility: What happens if you give key A away? That is, *really* give it away. Make key A public. Publish it on your web page. Hand it out at parties. Publish it on the back page of your book. Upload it to a public key repository. Write it backward on your forehead so it appears forward in the rear-view mirror of the guy you're tailgating. Let anyone, anyone at all, use that key.

Public-Key Encryption

No problem. The only possible use for that key is to encrypt messages that can be unencrypted only with the matching key that you kept or to decrypt messages encrypted by your key. People can encrypt messages that only you can read and can decrypt messages that only you could have sent. This is the whole basis behind *public-key encryption.* The published key is called the *public key,* whereas the key you keep is the *private key.* Together, a public key (key A) and its corresponding private key (key B) are called a *keypair.*

Every OpenPGP user has a personal keypair, with the public key disseminated widely and the private key kept as a closely guarded secret. OpenPGP provides methods to broadcast the public key to the world because body tattoos are neither necessary nor desirable in cryptography.

Although OpenPGP uses passphrases (as discussed later in this chapter) to make private key theft more difficult than simply stealing a file from your computer, there's no reason to make it easy for Mallory. Anyone who has the private key and your passphrase can pretend to be you. Protect both of them! Throughout this book, we discuss ways to keep your private key private and make your public key more public.

Digital Signatures

When you digitally sign an unencrypted message, you allow anyone to read the contents of the message. The digital signature tells the recipient only that the sender had access to the matching private key for the public key he has for that person. Digital signatures use both hashes and public-key cryptography. They provide nonrepudiation and integrity, but not confidentiality. If you want everyone in the world to know you wrote something, a digital signature will do the trick.

You saw earlier that when someone alters a message, the hash for that message changes dramatically, which provides a simple check of the message's integrity. If you provide the message's hash in an email itself, there's a problem: Anyone who can change the email can also change the hash to match the new message. We need a technique to protect the hash from tampering. Our solution is to use public-key cryptography to digitally sign our message. Here are the basic steps the Open-PGP software performs after you tell it to sign your message:

1. Generates a hash of your message.

2. Encrypts the hash with your private key (your digital signature).

3. Attaches the encrypted hash to your message (this is your signed message).

4. Sends your message with the attachment.

The recipient will get an email message containing the message you sent in cleartext, plus a small attachment containing the encrypted hash. The recipient does not need to use OpenPGP to read the message, so it's less hassle to read the message than it would be to read a fully encrypted message.

By the same token, if the recipient has OpenPGP tools installed, the message's hash can be decrypted with your public key to get the hash of the message you sent. Because only you hold your private key, only you could have created that hash. The recipient can then independently generate the hash of the message that was received. If the two hashes match, the recipient can be certain that what is read is what you sent.

If someone tampers with your original message, anyone who tries to confirm the hash gets an error. Your public key might not decrypt the hash, which would indicate that some other person's private key created the message. Or your public key might decrypt the hash, but the hash would fail to match the hash for the email message received, telling the recipient that the email message was altered.

Combining Signatures and Asymmetric Cryptography

We discussed hashes, which show whether a document has been tampered with. We also covered public-key cryptography: An asymmetric cipher allows people to encrypt messages for a particular person, or a person can send messages that could have come only from him. Digital signatures combine both of these ideas, but OpenPGP takes them a step further. By combining the sender's private key and the recipient's public key, an OpenPGP message can be read only by its intended audience and could have come only from a particular sender, as shown in Figure 1-1.

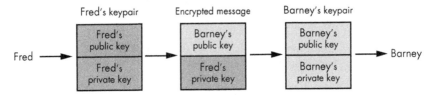

Figure 1-1: OpenPGP keys and an encrypted message

As you can see in Figure 1-1, both Fred and Barney have keypairs that consist of a public and a private key. These people have never communicated before; instead, their public keys are available on the Internet. Each of them has kept the private key secret.

When Fred wants to send a message to Barney, Fred signs the message with his private key and encrypts it with Barney's public key. The encryption can only be undone by someone who has Barney's private key, and the signature can only be verified by someone who has Fred's public key.

By using both a private key and a public key from two different people, we ensure that anyone who wants to read the message and verify its authenticity must have Fred's public key and Barney's private key. Fred's public key is easy to find, but Barney's private key is a closely-held secret. The *only* person who has *both* of these keys is Barney.

NOTE *Not even Fred has both of the necessary keys; he lacks Barney's private key. Once the message is encrypted, even the sender cannot decrypt it!*

This simple aspect of OpenPGP has secured the lives of dissidents and relief workers in totalitarian, oppressive governments and war-torn areas.

Passphrases and Private Keys

OpenPGP private keys (and those in many other programs, such as Secure Shell) have two components: a file on your disk and a *passphrase*. The file on disk contains your private key, scrambled and shredded beyond recovery. A passphrase is much like a password, except that it is much longer and includes spaces. Whenever you work with your private key, the OpenPGP program will request your passphrase. OpenPGP combines the passphrase you enter with the private key file saved on disk to reassemble a working private key. If you enter the wrong passphrase, this private key is wrong and will not work. Thus, a stolen laptop containing a private key file will be useless to the person who finds it, unless you save your passphrase in a plain text file somewhere, that is! *The only safe place for your passphrase is in your head.*

Choosing a Passphrase

Computers are now so fast that they can crack short passwords rapidly simply by trying each possible password in quick succession. This process is called *brute forcing.* Although you can use a simple password for a passphrase, doing so considerably reduces the security of your private key. Your passphrase should be at least several words long, it should be something you can easily remember, and it shouldn't be obvious to others. Work special characters such as #, !, ~, and so on into your passphrase. Peculiar words used in your professional vocabulary are also a good choice. Substitute numbers for letters. If you work with computers, you can use computer shorthand, such as substituting "|" for "or." Confuse upper- and lowercase. Do not use catch phrases, tag lines, or bits from popular books or movies as your passphrase! Although "He's dead, Jim" might be very easy for you to remember, it's both easy to guess and far too short.

Many people recommend combining all the above into a passphrase. You can start with a phrase such as "He's dead, Jim" and expand on it: "On the first Star Trek series, McCoy said 'He's dead, Jim' in far, far too many episodes!" is a far better start for a passphrase[2] and is probably unique. Other experts recommend starting with a few sentences from an obscure book. If you know a foreign language, even slightly, substitute some of the foreign words for English equivalents. That useless degree in 17th century French literature is an excellent source for passphrases that will be extremely difficult to either guess or brute force.

After you have a base passphrase, fold, spindle, and mutilate it with special characters and weird substitutions. Add in your special characters, illiterate punctuation, and whatever other changes you desire. Make it longer and more complicated for better security. Your final passphrase should be meaningless to anyone except you.

---

[2] This might have been an acceptable place to start with passphrase creation, but now that it's published as such, it's a really lousy one.

Here's the scariest bit about public-key cryptography: *Anyone who has your complete private key can pretend to be you.* If someone steals your laptop and understands OpenPGP, the person can assume your electronic identity if he can get your complete OpenPGP private key. Your OpenPGP private key consists of numbers in a file on your computer's hard drive and your passphrase. You can only protect that file so well; by choosing a solid passphrase, you make your key much harder for anyone else to use.

After you begin using OpenPGP regularly to secure your personal information, losing your private key is like losing your wallet, credit cards, passport, and birth certificate simultaneously. And in some parts of the world, digital signatures are legally binding. Your boss might get that threatening email, and you couldn't repudiate it. You might learn one day that you've apparently agreed to open a warehouse-style, discount mail-order bride distribution center in Kansas. The passphrase is your key to peace of mind; choose it well.

If you use OpenPGP to protect personal documents, you might choose to record your passphrase somewhere so that a family member could get it in case of your untimely demise. This is a personal choice; although a safe deposit box might not be as secure as you want, it's much better than relying on the IRS to provide accurate copies of your financial records to your spouse after your death. It is perfectly reasonable to have shared OpenPGP keypairs used by family members to protect family financial documents. Many teams use just such an approach for a group key, as will be discussed in Chapter 11.

Now that you understand some of the basics of cryptography as used in OpenPGP, let's examine the way OpenPGP itself hangs together.

2

UNDERSTANDING OPENPGP

Now that you understand the ideas behind basic encryption, what makes OpenPGP so special? Aside from the decade-old lawsuit that freed up US encryption export regulations, what happened to make the computing world give OpenPGP so much attention? After all, the cryptography underlying OpenPGP has been widely deployed in a variety of applications and protocols, so that's not the secret.

OpenPGP's secret is also what might be its most exciting part: the whole concept of the Web of Trust. To use OpenPGP well, you need to understand the Web of Trust.

This chapter introduces the ideas behind the Web of Trust and some considerations when creating and using public and private keys. We will discuss the details of managing the Web of Trust in Chapter 5, and will specifically cover PGP in Chapter 6 and GnuPG in Chapter 7.

Security and OpenPGP

Let's consider the word *security* for a moment. This is one of those poor innocent words that's been kicked around until it means just about anything the speaker wants it to. OpenPGP provides some things that we normally think of as security, but it's really a very limited subset of the whole world of security.

OpenPGP won't keep someone from stealing your computer. It won't stop someone from sending you three million junk emails. It does provide confidentiality, integrity, and non-repudiation, but its implementation of these are all tightly tied to and derived from the idea of *identity*.

One can argue that the idea driving OpenPGP is identity verification. Identifying people in person is pretty easy—humans have done that with their five senses for tens of thousands of years, and we've gotten pretty good at it. Identifying the sender of an email is more difficult. When you receive an email message, the only information with which to identify the sender is an easily-forged "From" address.

When you receive a message signed with someone else's private key, however, you can rest assured that it almost certainly came from the person with the matching private key. The question then becomes, "How do you tie a real-world identity to the keypair?" This has long been the killer problem in public-key cryptography.

Big companies take a big-scale approach to this problem. Secure Sockets Layer (SSL) websites use digital certificates issued by Certificate Authority (CA) companies that (in theory) spend a lot of time verifying the identity of the person or company requesting the certificate. This is a time-consuming process that costs a good amount of money to do correctly. After a website owner convinces the CA that he is who he claims to be, the CA digitally signs the website's public key, which is the CA's proclamation that it has verified the identity of the certificate holder.

This approach, although basically decent, has weaknesses. First, any business expects to be paid. I don't want to pay some company 100 dollars every year or two just to prove my email identity—that's more expensive than my driver's license! What's more, even these big CAs can be tricked into signing invalid certificate requests, so you're not getting an ironclad guarantee of validity.

In fact, the digital signature used by a CA doesn't differ in any technological or cryptographic sense from the digital signatures you can create with your own private key.

The key difference between OpenPGP and a central CA is that OpenPGP allows you to create digital signatures yourself.

The Web of Trust abolishes the whole idea of a central CA and places the responsibility for identity verification in the hands of the users.

NOTE *The general design of the X.509 certificates used on websites does differ from the OpenPGP keypair. The two are not interchangeable because they use different algorithms and include different information, but the underlying technology is the same (much as a convertible and a pickup resemble each other).*

Web of Trust

The Web of Trust is the global network of people who have identified each other and digitally signed each other's Open-PGP keys. The Web of Trust is composed entirely of links between individuals. Over the years, as more and more people have joined the Web of Trust, the network has become broader and more interconnected. Everyone who is using OpenPGP to communicate with a variety of people is connected via the Web of Trust.

For example, suppose that at some point I receive a digitally signed email from George. I have never met George, but I can get a copy of George's public key from a central repository. This key has been digitally signed by people who have verified his identity.

One of these signers is William, whom I do know. I trust William to not have signed George's key unless he either knows George personally or has verified his identity in some other way. When I verify William's signature of George's key, I know that William really does "vouch" that George is George. I trust William, and William trusts George, so I can trust that George is George. And this chain can continue to grow. Perhaps I trust William, who trusts Larry, who trusts Betty, who trusts Ivan, who trusts George, and so on. That's the web.

As George has his key signed by more and more people, his key is more tightly integrated into the Web of Trust and the average length of the path to his key becomes shorter and shorter.

The Web of Trust is not perfect. I might trust William's ability to check identity when signing keys, but I don't know anything about George's; maybe he signs the keys of anyone he meets, or signs keys he randomly downloads from the Open-PGP keyservers. If we were going to start over with OpenPGP today, the Web of Trust would look completely different. Just remember that ultimately, you decide who you trust. You can always refuse to sign a key, or refuse to accept identity because of a too-distant connection to someone you trust.

Trust in OpenPGP

Like so many other words in the security field, *trust* has
been twisted to mean almost anything the speaker desires.
(The OpenPGP standard actually goes out of its way to avoid
defining the word *trust*!) One critical portion of the trust system is the Web of Trust, which uses a narrow definition of trust
and tries to ensure only that a person is who he claims he is.

Simply being a part of the Web of Trust does not imply that
a person is trustworthy! I know people whom I know darn well
that I cannot trust with my wallet or my pet rats, but I would
happily sign their PGP keys and help them prove their identity
to others. You can receive an OpenPGP-signed email containing a fraudulent offer to sell the Brooklyn Bridge at pennies on
the dollar; if the sender's key is attached to the Web of Trust,
you have at least a chance of identifying him.

The responsibility for building this trust is in your hands.
Collecting other OpenPGP users' digital signatures on your
key, and signing their keys in return, is an important part of
using OpenPGP. You should be as tightly meshed into the Web
of Trust as humanly possible.

By the same token, it would be unfair to say that "the more
signatures you have on your key, the more your key will be
trusted." Lots of signatures do not ensure that the key will be
universally trusted. On the other hand, the more hops between
you and another user in the Web of Trust, and the fewer paths
between the two of you, the less likely that person will be to trust
your identity. (See "Tracing the Web of Trust" on page 121.)

By signing someone else's key, you are stating publicly that
you have identified this person, and you are satisfied that his
identity matches the identity provided with his public key. Likewise, to get your key signed by someone else, you must prove
your identity to him. Many people assume that a government-
issued ID such as a passport or driver's license suffices as proof
of identity.

This might seem like a weak system, but it's no weaker
than the one used by a central CA. The CA is staffed by human
beings just like you, after all. Although these staff members
have training to detect false IDs, they have limitations simply
because they work remotely. If a person is standing in front of
you with her driver's license, you can look at her picture and
compare it with her face. The CA has no such option.

Also, most of us check identification rarely enough that
its very novelty means we probably pay enough attention to
do a decent job at it. Those folks who work for a CA check IDs
all day long, every day. I remember more than one Monday
morning at work when I was less careful and less productive

than my employer would hope.[1] Although anyone could get a forged ID card if they knew who to talk to, they can fool a CA almost as easily as they can fool you. Just look at the people who work for the TSA; they check ID cards all day long and quickly become bored with the routine.

Of course, you won't be able to verify all state-issued ID cards. If I meet someone who uses a Tasmanian passport, I'm going to hesitate over signing his key unless he has some other method of proving his identity. (Tasmania is a state within Australia, and doesn't issue its own passports. If you didn't know this, don't blindly trust government-issued IDs!) You're perfectly within your rights to only sign keys for people you know well. Many experienced OpenPGP users follow this strategy; don't be offended if they won't sign your key based solely on your state ID. I won't sign your key unless I know you.

One common way to enhance your links into the Web of Trust is to attend a keysigning party. At a keysigning party, OpenPGP users gather to verify each other's identity and sign each other's keys. Keysigning parties are usually held at technical conferences and occasionally at other events where a large number of tech-literate people have gathered.

If you have never heard of a keysigning party and don't want to go looking for one, ask your friends and inquire around your place of work. In any community of technically oriented people, at least one person has an OpenPGP keypair. Some social networking sites, such as www.biglumber.com, exist primarily to match people up to exchange signatures on OpenPGP keys.

A single signature attaches you to the Web of Trust. After you start using OpenPGP you'll be surprised at how many other people also use it.

Where to Install

An OpenPGP program provides an affidavit that you are who you claim you are, like your driver's license or a notary's stamp. And, just as you wouldn't leave your driver's license lying around at the public library, you shouldn't use OpenPGP on any computer you do not completely control. Other users on the same computer might be able to access your keyring, including your ultrasecret private key. Even if you have the permissions set on your keys so that only you can see them, don't forget that people with administrative access to the system can access those files anyway. This means that you shouldn't install OpenPGP on a shared system, such as those in the university computer lab.

---

[1] Note to the boss: Those days were all at previous jobs. This never happens now. Really.

Don't install it on a communal office terminal. The coffee shop terminal is Right Out. Although I read my email on a shared server, when I use any OpenPGP program I compose the mail on my laptop and upload it to my mail server.

Your personal computer should also be well-secured; if you leave your computer in the office and have no locking screen saver, people could access your keys.

Now let's talk about Windows. Versions of Windows descended from Windows 95 (including Windows 98 and Windows Me) aren't true multiuser operating systems; their multiuser functionality is bolted on rather than integrated throughout the system. You cannot successfully secure Open-PGP keys on a multiuser Windows 9x system; anyone who uses that system could access your keys without you ever knowing about it. The password functionality in these versions of Windows is easily bypassed by anyone who can touch the system, without any special tools or software. As such, I recommend against storing any personal information, including OpenPGP keys, on Windows 9x systems.

Windows NT–based operating systems such as Windows Vista, Windows XP, and Windows 2000 are much improved in this regard; breaking into them requires special software tools and time, just like a Unix-like system. On the other hand, they do have that pesky Administrator account that can install anything it likes. Just like a Unix-like "root" account, you must be certain that nobody else can access your keyring.

We'll touch on this topic, but an in-depth look is beyond the scope of this book. If you're interested in desktop computer security, there are many books on the market that deal specifically with that topic.

Your Keypair

No matter which version of OpenPGP you choose to use, you have to create a keypair when you install the software. The steps for doing so will differ, but both sets of software use the same underlying ideas. Again, see Chapter 3 for specific PGP instructions and Chapter 4 for GnuPG instructions.

NOTE *Remember to generate your keys only on a machine that only you control. If you leave your GnuPG keypair lying around for anyone to use, that anyone can pretend to be you!*

Key Length

The *key length* is the number of bits (zeros and ones) in your keypair. At the time of this writing, both PGP and GnuPG default to 2048-bit keys. A 2048-bit symmetric key suffices to provide robust security for the next several years, unless your attacker has quantum computers or one of those ultrasecret custom-built, code-busting machines the NSA is rumored to have.

Increasing the key size increases the amount of work needed to process your key—not just the amount of work needed to send encrypted emails but also the amount of work others must do to *read* them. It also increases the amount of work the bad guys have to do to break your key, however. Stick with the defaults, unless you know that everyone you will ever exchange encrypted messages with has sufficient computing power to decrypt your messages without having to take a coffee break while the machine churns.

Key Expiration Date

The expiration date of a keypair is a matter of discussion among OpenPGP experts. Having a key expire regularly provides a certain level of additional convenience for your future self; if you leave your nonexpiring keypair on a CD-ROM, and someone finds that disk in 2038, they can still use that keypair to pretend to be you. If your key expires regularly, you will need to generate a new key every few years and distribute it amongst your correspondents.

As a new OpenPGP user, however, you will probably find things that you wish you had done differently with your key before too long. If your key lasts forever, it will be more difficult to get rid of. I recommend that you have your first key expire in a year. You can probably have subsequent keys expire every two to five years, but you want to be able to bail out of any teething problems quickly. (Although I've done my best to guide you through any potential problems, some of you will find uses for OpenPGP that I'd never expect!)

Perhaps the most common problem with a nonexpiring key is that when an old key is used to contact someone who no longer has the keypair, they can't read the email. If I had publicized a nonexpiring PGP key when I first gave PGP a try back in 1995, that key would still be available via Google and other websites. Chances are, today I would have had to scrounge hard to dig up the software to read a message encrypted with that key. And in 2015, I would have serious difficulty opening that message, but the key would still be cached for the world at large to view, and no matter how hard I worked to publicize an updated expiring key, people would keep tripping over the old one!

The moral of this story is: *Expire your keys regularly!*

Name, Email, and Comment

Your name, your email address, and an optional comment field combine to create your OpenPGP user ID, or UID. You must be very careful to enter these in the most correct manner to get the greatest possible use out of OpenPGP.

Your Name

Use your *real name*. Remember, one important part of using GnuPG is getting people to sign your public key. Although it's easy to get your friends and family to sign your keys, proving your identity to strangers so that they will sign your keys is a little more difficult.

The best way to get your key signed is to provide some sort of government-issued ID with your name on it. My passport says "Michael Warren Lucas Jr.," my books are authored by "Michael W. Lucas," my company email account lists me as "Michael Lucas," and my coworkers have still other names for me. (Because I want this book to avoid an R rating, I won't mention those names here.) If I'm trying to prove my identity to someone I've never met before, it's best if my key matches the name on my government-issued identification as closely as possible.

Email Address

You also need an email address. Your key is tied to an email address, for better or worse.

Comment

The *comment* is just a few words about who you are and what you do. This can be important because many people have similar names. If I perform a Google search for "Michael Lucas" I find a whole bunch of interesting characters: voiceover artists, actors, firearm instructors, ministers, and so on. Although I wish them all well, I don't want anyone to try to negotiate my book contract with them (because my publisher is such a bastard, he'll take them for all they're worth). The comment field allows me to differentiate myself, so that if anyone else goes looking for the OpenPGP key for a random "Michael Lucas" I won't get unreadable mail intended for someone else.

User ID

This triple identifier of name, email address, and comment is called a *user ID*, or *UID*. UIDs are expected to refer to a unique entity. When someone goes looking for your private key, they won't want to find it by a string of meaningless characters; they want to use your name! If they can't remember your full name, they'll want to use your email address.

Although it's unlikely that someone wanting to reach me would search for my public key by the fact that I'm an author, it would help sort me out from all the other Michael Lucases in the world who might use OpenPGP.

Revocation Certificates

A *revocation certificate* allows you to announce to the world that your keypair is no longer valid. You need a revocation certificate if your private key is lost, compromised, or stolen. You might also forget your passphrase, which would lock you out of your own private key and render you unable to read any encrypted messages you receive.

You might even lose the technology to read your keypair! Occasionally, you will hear about some user who receives an email encrypted with a PGP key dating from 1992, in a format that no modern OpenPGP-compliant program can read. (This is perhaps the most important reason why your key should expire!) In any of these cases, you'll want to be able to "shut off" your old key.

Generate a revocation certificate immediately upon generating a key.

Storing Your Keypair

After you start using OpenPGP, losing your private key (or the whole keypair) will cause you no end of grief. I've had files disappear due to user error, filesystem bugs destroy data I didn't realize was important until weeks later, and operating system bugs render machines unbootable. Three of my machines have caught on fire. Unlike the corporate world, in which you can always blame goofs on the IT department, you are the only person who can protect your OpenPGP keys. You cannot delegate this responsibility.

Back up your keypair and your revocation certificate on a portable medium, such as a CD-ROM or floppy disk, and store it in a safe place such as a safe deposit box. Perhaps carry it with you, encrypted, on a USB key.

A safe is not a bad choice, but although a fireproof safe won't get hot enough to ignite paper it will get more than hot enough to corrupt digital media. You can also print out your revocation certificate and store it with the digital backup, so that if your backup media fails with age you could still hand-copy the revocation certificate and revoke your key if necessary.

Do not store your keypair and/or revocation certificate on a public machine, semipublic machine, or shared machine! Yes, I've said this before, but it bears repeating until it sinks in.

Storing Your Revocation Certificate

Just as anyone who gets your private key and passphrase can pass himself off as you, anyone who gets your revocation certificate can make your private key unusable by the world at large. This would be annoying for a novice, but if you use OpenPGP heavily it would be catastrophic. Store your revocation certificate just as securely as you store your private key.

Photo IDs and OpenPGP Keys

One of the more recent additions to OpenPGP is the ability to store a picture in a public key. This makes verifying key owners much more reliable, as you can actually view a picture when you're deciding whether or not to sign a key. It also gives you a better "feel" for the person.

Both PGP and GnuPG can extract and display photos in keys.

If you want to insert your own photo into your key, you'll need to have a digital photo of yourself in either a head-only or head-and-shoulders shot. For best results, it should be 120x144 pixels and in JPEG format—this will work in both PGP and GnuPG. Key size is a critical issue in OpenPGP, so your photo should take up as little space as possible: It doesn't need to be super-detailed so long as people can recognize you. After all, how many driver's licenses have decent photographs?

Inserting a photo into your public key isn't hard, but it does require slightly more advanced skills than you have right now. We will discuss managing photo ID in Chapters 6 (for PGP) and 7 (for GnuPG).

Key Distribution

Putting your public key on your web page might seem like the obvious thing to do, but this only demonstrates that the obvious choice isn't always the best. Anyone can put up a website claiming to be "The Official Website of Michael W. Lucas!" Anyone could put a public key on that site. Worse, anyone could put a note on that web page saying "To reach the internationally-renowned author of *PGP & GPG*, as well as many other fine tomes of computer wisdom, email him at michaellucastheauthor@hotmail.com and use this OpenPGP key!" (Of course, that isn't my website, my email address, or my OpenPGP key. Anyone trusting that will find themselves talking to someone else—and blaming me for the results.)

At times, you'll see email signatures with the line "My public key is available at http://www.mywebsite.com/," which seems like it would be better. It's certainly so popular that you'd think it would work. If someone tampered with the email, however, they could also put in a new URL for the public key website and fool the recipient. This works best when the author sends a lot of email, so correspondents can verify the URL with that displayed in other messages. This would work well only with people who know me and would be disturbed if I suddenly started using a different email provider.

Unquestionably, the best way to distribute your key is in person. When a coworker sets up an OpenPGP keypair, I have him email the public key to me, we verify it together, and then I add it to my keyring.

This simply doesn't scale, however—you can't go tracking down public keys for everyone in the world! There's also a certain recursive problem in sending an email to get a key to verify the authenticity of an email you just received.

Fortunately, OpenPGP has a key distribution method that covers the whole world.

Keyservers

OpenPGP has special Internet servers designed specifically for handling and sharing OpenPGP keys. These *keyservers* are much like other Internet servers that are customized to handle web pages, email, or any other protocol. OpenPGP includes hooks to automatically communicate with OpenPGP-compatible keyservers.

There are many, many keyservers throughout the world. Most of them replicate their key databases back and forth, ensuring that everyone's keys will be available upon demand.

Traditional OpenPGP keyservers allowed anyone to upload a key for any email address. This was great when the Internet was a more trusting place, but today it isn't as useful. The PGP Corporation provides a "verified PGP key" service, in which you can upload a key and send an approval email to the address in the key. Only the key owner can approve that key for listing in the keyserver, which provides a certain level of authorization—Mallory must control the email account of a person he wants to spoof a key for, and if he can do that then OpenPGP won't do anything to stop him anyhow.

Before sending your public key to the world, be certain that you have made the proper preparations to use OpenPGP. Back up your public and private keys. Create a revocation certificate. Store the whole mess in a safe place. Failing to do these things might result in your posting an "orphaned" key to the world, which means that you will receive encrypted (and presumably important) email that you cannot read. If in doubt, don't put your key on a keyserver for a little while. You can always upload it later.

Keyservers are not the be-all and end-all of public key distribution. It doesn't hurt to put your public key on your website; if nothing else, it provides one more level of confirmation of a key's accuracy for those people sufficiently paranoid to check.

Many users with accounts on shared Unix-like systems put their public key in their finger text or plan for other system users to see. These methods are perfectly fine as add-ons but don't integrate well with the OpenPGP infrastructure. Your average OpenPGP user won't want to track down the web page of a correspondent—she wants her email client to simply go to a keyserver and grab the key!

Some people choose to not use keyservers for their own reasons. Perhaps they don't want to receive OpenPGP-encrypted mail from random people or they have fundamental architectural disagreements with the security of the keyserver system. These people publicize their keys with their own preferred methods, and you'll have to jump through the hoops they've devised to communicate with them.

People can and do have legitimate concerns about the reliability and integrity of the keyserver system; they're an example of something that was implemented before the Internet became so popular and that we now have to live with. If OpenPGP were implemented from scratch today, we would probably use something different, but the same can be said for the Web, for email, and for all the other protocols that make the Internet what it is today. However, keyservers are a far better system than the Internet's default, which is to provide no means of verifying authenticity.

Now that you know what the software you chose will be doing, let's see how to install both PGP and GnuPG.

3

INSTALLING PGP

PGP Corporation produces several different types of PGP software, from PGP Desktop to PGP Command Line, and several different enterprise-level products. We'll focus on the desktop PGP software useful for most people. To an end user, all the versions behave similarly; they all implement

the OpenPGP standard, after all! The various desktop products do have slightly different features, however, and you should take those features into consideration when purchasing the software. For example, as of this writing PGP has two "desktop" versions: Home and Professional. The Home version provides basic email features, whereas Professional gives you the ability to encrypt your entire hard drive as well. Choose the version whose features best suit your needs.

Downloading PGP

To begin, download PGP from the company website, www.pgp
.com. (I won't provide an exact URL, mainly because web
designers seem to make a habit of redesigning their websites
within a week of one of my books going to press!) PGP provides a free 30-day trial of its "home desktop" software, as well
as the option to purchase immediately. The 30-day trial isn't a
bad way to get a taste without laying down cash for the privilege. If you like it, you can buy a license code on the website.

Within a day or two of your order, you'll receive an email
that includes a link to where you can download the software, a
list of instructions, and license numbers. Keep this email! Not
only will you need this information to install PGP, you will also
need it if you require support. Each PGP download and license
key is specific to the person who ordered it: It has the user's
name, email address, and so on hard-coded into it. This means
that if I order PGP for my wife, I must put her name, her email
address, and her other information on the order form. If I put
my information in the download form, the software will be
licensed for my use instead of hers and will not work.

The download includes a typical Windows installation EXE
file. Double-click it to get started.

Installing PGP

The installer begins with a typical license screen. Read
this carefully and agree if you want to continue the install.
You'll then see a pop-up that contains the release notes, and
describes all the features and integration supported by this version of PGP. After a typical sliding blue bar shows you the files
being installed, you'll be asked to reboot. After the reboot, log
into the user account in which you intend to use PGP, and a
pop-up window will ask if you want to use PGP. Say Yes.

The Licensing Assistant confirms that you have a valid PGP
license. Enter your name, organization, and email address
exactly as you entered them in the order form. (If you forgot, they're included in the email with your license code.)
Figure 3-1 shows a sample of the PGP Licensing Assistant.

The next window asks for your license code. As of this
writing, the license code is a 28-character alphanumeric string
included in your order form. You can also request a 30-day
evaluation, purchase a full license, or use the program without
a license in a crippled mode. (Using PGP without a license
allows you to access files that you have previously encrypted,
but not much else.) Enter your license key and continue.

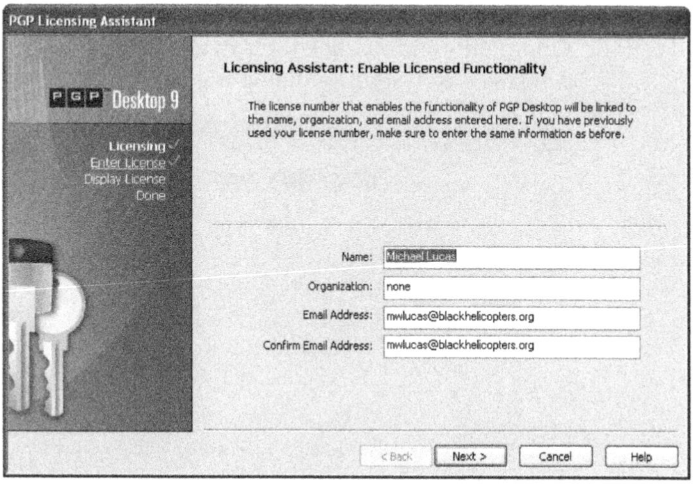

Figure 3-1: The PGP Licensing Assistant

After PGP validates your license key, you'll be asked if you're a new user or if you want to import previous PGP keys. Select **New User**, and PGP will begin the key generation process. The first screen of the PGP Setup Assistant requests your full name and your primary email address, as shown in Figure 3-2.

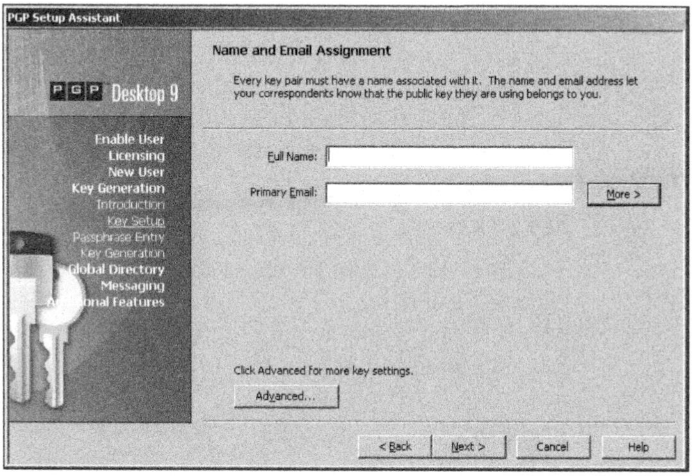

Figure 3-2: The Name and Email Assignment screen

The More button and the Advanced button are important. If you have more than one email account that you want to secure with PGP, select **More** to create more space to list email addresses.

If you're planning to communicate only with people who use official PGP, Inc. software, you're all set. However, if you

want to use OpenPGP with anyone who uses software from any
OpenPGP vendor, click the **Advanced** button. You'll see the
Advanced Key Settings dialog box, as shown in Figure 3-3.

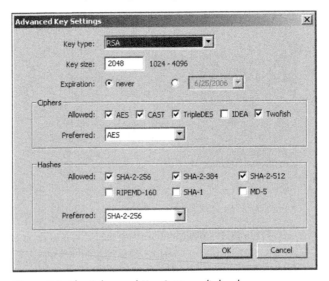

Figure 3-3: The Advanced Key Settings dialog box

Key Type

OpenPGP supports many different types of keys, including keys
that are valid for signing messages but not encrypting them,
keys compatible with older versions of OpenPGP, and so on.
The modern standard for average email use is RSA.

Key Size

This is the key length in bits, as discussed in "Your Keypair" on
page 32. The default is 2048 and should be sufficient for most
people. Longer keypairs are useful only if your data should
remain confidential decades or centuries from now.

Expiration

Choose whether to have your key expire at a certain time (as
discussed in Chapter 2) or to never expire. I recommend that
you set an expiration date no more than one year in the future,
at least on your first keypair.

Ciphers

Remember from Chapter 1 that a cipher is a method
of encrypting text. PGP presents a list of ciphers it will

understand, including Advanced Encryption Standard (AES), Cast, TripleDES, IDEA, and Twofish. The differences between these ciphers are generally only of interest to cryptographers; today, almost everyone uses AES. The "preferred" cipher is the one your software will use by default when composing messages. Almost everyone composes messages in AES today, and everyone with modern software can read it; it is best to leave it as your preferred cipher.

One thing that sets PGP apart from other OpenPGP implementations is that it can use the IDEA cipher, but today's PGP doesn't understand IDEA by default. If you want to read IDEA-protected messages, you must check its box on the list here.

Hashes

Different OpenPGP implementations support different hash algorithms. (We discussed hashes in Chapter 1.) Each of the algorithms listed here is just a different way to generate hashes. Checking the boxes for additional hash algorithms doesn't mean that you'll use them when composing messages, but it does mean that PGP will understand messages sent using these algorithms. Some of these hashes are older, weaker, and effectively broken, so you must choose what to support. For maximum security, select everything but MD5 and SHA-1. For maximum compatibility, including compatibility with messages sent by older software using these older, weaker algorithms, select all the hashes. Click **OK** to continue with the install and bring up the Passphrase Assignment screen, shown in Figure 3-4.

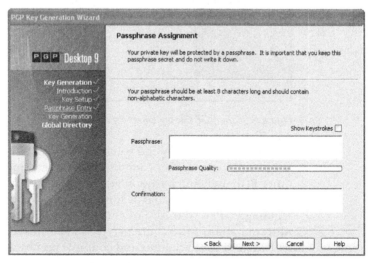

Figure 3-4: The Passphrase Assignment screen

The Passphrase Assignment screen is where you'll enter your all-important passphrase. As discussed in Chapter 1, a good passphrase is a fundamental part of using PGP. To help you choose a good passphrase, a green bar will scroll across the middle of the screen in the Passphrase Quality bar as you type your passphrase. If your passphrase is good enough for average use, the green will fill the entire space provided. Choose a good passphrase and secure it as discussed in Chapter 1.

PGP then generates your key. You'll see pretty flashing lights on the screen to assure you that the computer is actually doing something as it computes a whole bunch of random numbers, strings them together, and calls them your key. When complete, you'll be asked to click **Next**.

The next screen offers to publish your public key using the PGP Global Directory Assistant, as shown in Figure 3-5. We're not quite ready to do that yet, so click **Skip**. (Although the official PGP corporate keyservers allow users to remove their own OpenPGP keys, it's best to have a revocation certificate before publishing the certificate anywhere!)

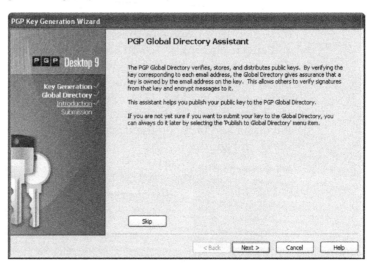

Figure 3-5: The PGP Global Directory Assistant

PGP then offers to find your email and AOL Instant Messenger accounts, so that communications between you and other PGP users will be automatically encrypted. Let it do so; it will save you the trouble of configuring these accounts later. (Adding PGP to your AIM or email accounts will not interfere with your ability to send unencrypted mail.) Just click **Next** to let PGP find your accounts and continue on its way.

The installer then displays the standard policies that determine when PGP will encrypt messages. We'll devote most of

Chapter 9 to PGP policies, so for now just click **Next** to finish the installation.

Congratulations! PGP is now installed on your computer. Next we'll back up your key for safety, and generate a revocation certificate so you can publish your PGP key.

PGP Key Backups

You manage all your PGP settings and perform most PGP tasks through the PGP Desktop, accessible under the Windows Start ▶ Programs menu. We'll begin by backing up your private key.

1. Open the PGP Desktop. You should see a desktop similar to Figure 3-6.

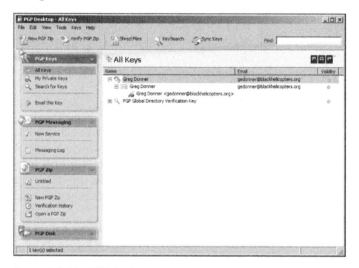

Figure 3-6: The PGP Desktop

2. You'll see two keys when you first start your desktop: the one generated during the install (for Greg Donner, in this example), and the PGP Global Directory Verification Key. (The latter, which is used by the PGP Corporation to verify keys, is included with all PGP installs.) Right-click your key and select **Export**.

3. A fairly standard Save pop-up window displays, as shown in Figure 3-7, with one exception: the **Include Private Key(s)** box in the lower-left corner. *You must check this box before saving in order to save your private key.* If you don't, you will be backing up only your public key, which is the same information that will be available on dozens of keyservers worldwide before long.

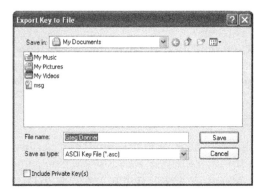

Figure 3-7: Saving an exported key

4. Save your private key and save the file. By default, saving
    creates a file using your name and a .asc extension under
    your My Documents folder. Back up this file somewhere,
    as discussed in Chapter 1, so if your machine is lost or
    destroyed you can access PGP-encrypted messages you
    will receive on your new computer.

Important Installation Locations

PGP stores its application data in your Application Data directory under a folder called PGP Corporation. Although the
install process set the permissions on this folder so that only
you can access it, be certain that you don't change it in the
course of day-to-day work. When you back up your system, be
sure to include this folder!

Similarly, PGP installs Registry keys under HKEY_LOCAL_
MACHINE/SOFTWARE/PGP Corporation. These Registry
keys are not user-configurable, but do be sure to include them
in your system backups.

Revocation Certificates and PGP

Remember from Chapter 2 that a revocation certificate allows
you to tell the world that your public key is no longer valid.
This is important if your computer is destroyed or your passphrase is stolen. If you are using PGP only to secure files on
your disk, and not to ever transmit encrypted data to others,
strictly speaking you do not require a revocation certificate.
Still, it is a good idea to generate a revocation certificate anyway, even though it's tedious and annoying. However, if you
will ever use PGP to send mail to other people, you *must* have a
revocation certificate.

PGP does allow you to revoke a key without the revocation certificate. This sounds like it eliminates the need for a revocation certificate, but it works only for keys stored on the PGP Global Directory. If you make your key available on any keyserver other than the PGP Global Directory, or if there is a possibility that someone else might make your key available on some other keyserver,[1] you must have a revocation certificate.

PGP allows you to have "designated revokers" who can send a revocation certificate on your behalf, but this is useful only in a corporate environment. I could choose to have a family member as a designated revoker, but if my computer is destroyed, it's entirely possible that theirs will be as well.

Generating a revocation certificate is a little bit tedious in PGP Desktop, but not unduly difficult. To generate a revocation certificate, you must disable automatic keyserver updates, confirm that your keypair is backed up, generate the revocation certificate, save the certificate, reinstall your keypair from the backup, and set the private key properties.

Disabling Keyserver Updates

As discussed in Chapter 2, a keyserver is a public repository of public keys. Before you generate a revocation certificate, be sure that your PGP install is not automatically sending updates to the keyserver; you don't want your revocation certificate sent to the keyserver immediately upon generation!

Begin with the PGP Options menu, as shown in Figure 3-8. (In PGP version 9, this is under the Tools menu.) Under the Keys tab, look for the Synchronization section and a checkbox called Automatically Synchronize Keys With Keyservers. Confirm that it is not checked.

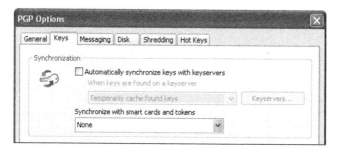

Figure 3-8: The PGP Options Keys tab with synchronization off

---

[1] Yes, it is rude to publicize someone else's public key. The world is full of rude people, and I rarely go wrong by assuming that someone will do something rude to my property.

Remember where this is because you'll want to turn it back on after we create the revocation certificate.

Revoke the Key

Now it's time to actually generate the revocation certificate. Before proceeding, be *absolutely* certain that you have backed up your key, including the private key, as discussed in "PGP Key Backups" on page 45. Generating the revocation certificate will make the keypair you have installed unusable, and you will need to restore the usable keypair from backup! If you're in any doubt whatsoever, back up your key again, *with* the private key.

To generate your revocation certificate:

1. Right-click your key in the PGP Desktop and select **Revoke**. You'll see a pop-up window that asks you to confirm that you want to revoke this key, as shown in Figure 3-9. Click **Yes**. A dialog box displays, asking for your passphrase (see Figure 3-10).

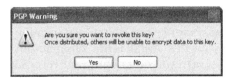

Figure 3-9: The PGP revocation warning

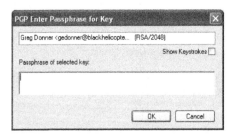

Figure 3-10: The PGP Passphrase dialog box

2. After you enter your passphrase, note that the entry for your key is in italics and no longer has a green dot by it. This key is revoked, at least in your PGP setup.

3. Now re-export the revoked key, just as described in "PGP Key Backups" on page 45. Be sure to export the private key as well. Give this backup a different name from your previous backup, however; do not overwrite your nonrevoked

key with your revoked key! This exported revoked key is your Revocation Certificate. Save it for later, and back it up in a safe place just like your other backup.

Now that you have a revocation certificate, delete the key. Go back to the PGP Desktop, right-click your key, and choose **Delete**. You will get two warnings, as shown in Figures 3-11 and 3-12. The first states that by deleting the private key, others will be able to encrypt messages to you that you won't be able to read. Because you have a backup of your private key, this isn't an issue. When you choose **OK**, PGP then warns you that deleting the private key is permanent and unrecoverable. If you don't have a backup, this is very true. You now have a PGP Desktop with only one key: the PGP Global Directory Verification Key.

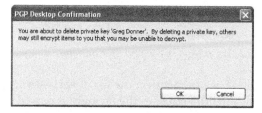

Figure 3-11: First private key deletion warning

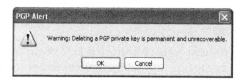

Figure 3-12: Second private key deletion warning

Re-import Your Private Key

To use your private key, you must re-import it.

1. Go to the **File** menu and select **Import**.

2. Select the backup that includes your private key. A pop-up appears, as shown in Figure 3-13, which asks you to select the key you want to import to your keyring. There's only one choice in this backup: your own. Select it and click **Import**.

You will see a pop-up window, warning you that you are importing private keys and that you need to assign the trust manually, as shown in Figure 3-14. Click **OK**.

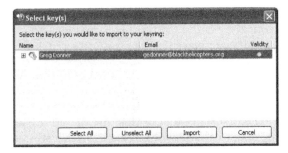

Figure 3-13: Choose a key to import.

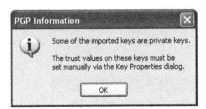

Figure 3-14: The private key import trust warning

Your key is now back on the list of keys—congratulations! Note that the little circle to the far right is grayed out, however; this key isn't valid at the moment. You need to manually tell PGP to trust this key.

Key Properties

To tell PGP to trust your re-imported key, begin by right-clicking the key listing and selecting **Properties** to bring up the key properties dialog box, in which you will make changes to your personal keys (see Figure 3-15). The options here allow you to change anything you want. You can make mistakes that will impair your ability to use PGP, however, so be very careful with what you do. Unless you know exactly what a field means and its implications for OpenPGP interoperability, it's strongly recommended to leave extra fields alone!

The function of many of the options here should be obvious: To add an email address or change your passphrase, click the appropriate box. You can change or remove an expiration date with the Expires tab, and so on. When restoring a private key from backup, we need the Trust field.

Trust indicates how much you trust the key, as discussed in Chapter 2. Because this is your private key, generated by you, you (hopefully!) trust it completely. Click the drop-down menu and change it to **Implicit**. This takes place immediately, without the need to click OK somewhere.

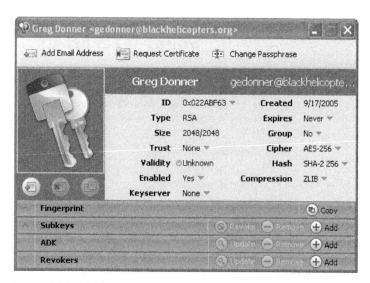

Figure 3-15: PGP key properties

Using the Revocation Certificate

If you forget your passphrase or if you believe that Mallory has compromised your key in some manner, import your revocation certificate and update the keyserver. This will publish the revocation certificate, and everyone who updates their copy of your key will get a notification that you have revoked your key.

Keyservers and PGP

Remember from Chapter 2 that a keyserver is a machine that provides a directory of OpenPGP keys. The PGP Corporation provides a keyserver for PGP users. This service works a little differently from other PGP keyservers in that it is email-verified.

When you install PGP, the software automatically submits your public key to the PGP Global Directory. As a verification step, the Global Directory sends an email to the address specified in the key; if you gave PGP the right email address, you'll receive that email. Clicking the link enclosed in the email will add your key to the Global Directory.

Unlike many other keyservers, the Global Directory does not share its keys with other keyservers, nor does it mirror data in other keyservers; it is considered a new, "clean" keyserver that lacks the decade-plus of cruft that has accumulated in other public keyservers. If you want to put your key in other keyservers, you will need to submit it to them separately.

OTHER PGP KEY DETAILS

I said you don't need to worry about the details of other fields in the PGP key properties screen, but some of you out there will wonder anyway. If not knowing things bugs you, here are the basics on what some of these other fields mean. Tampering with any of them is a good way to make your OpenPGP key unusable. You have been warned.

ID is your OpenPGP keyid.

Type is the cipher used in this key. The modern standard for average users is RSA.

Size is the number of bits in the key.

Keyserver allows you to assign a preferred keyserver for this key.

Expires lets you set or change an expiration date for this key.

Group lets you state whether this key is used by a group of people. (We'll discuss keys for groups in Chapter 11.)

Cipher lets you choose the algorithm this PGP key prefers to use.

Hash lets you choose the hash method this PGP key prefers to use.

Compression lets you choose the compression method this PGP key prefers.

Note that there is a Change Passphrase button in the Key Properties screen, which you can use without damaging your key.

To submit your key to the older keyserver hierarchy, find a website that takes key submissions. One that has been running for many years is http://pgpkeys.mit.edu, and a similar service is available at many sites in http://subkeys.pgp.net. If that site is down, a Google search for *submit PGP key* will bring up any number of keyservers that provide this service.

After you locate your keyserver, right-click your key in PGP Desktop. You'll see an option to **Copy Public Key**. Select this option to copy the public key into the system clipboard, then paste it into the web submission form. You're done—not too hard, was it?

Congratulations! You finished setting up PGP. Although PGP involves a lot of nitpicky details, compare the size of this chapter to the size of the next and be grateful that you're getting off easier than the GnuPG people.

4

INSTALLING GNUPG

GnuPG is freely available via the Internet, and you can get a variety of ready-to-use versions for any number of operating systems, source code, customized versions, and add-ons in a whole variety of places. Although GnuPG itself is extremely reliable, some of these add-ons and versions might not offer the quality you hope for. Getting the right software, installing it properly, and configuring it suitably will prevent a lot of problems later.

We'll begin by discussing the easiest-to-use versions of GnuPG—precompiled binaries—and proceed to the more obscure and unusual variants of the software.

You might find that the information you need appears early in this chapter. If that's the case, feel free to read only what you need and skip the rest. This is especially applicable if you're a Windows user who is not interested in building GnuPG from source code.

The official home of GnuPG on the Internet is www.GnuPG.org. Consider this the master authoritative source of GnuPG programs, code, and information. If you read anything that conflicts with information at this website, chances are that the website is correct and the outside document is wrong. (Because GnuPG is undergoing constant development and this book is static, the website even overrides the book you're reading now!)

Downloading GnuPG

To download a copy of GnuPG, start at the main website and follow the Download link. This link takes you to a page containing links for various Unix-like operating systems as well as Windows. (You can choose to download from a *mirror site* instead of the main site, which will reduce the load on the main server and will almost certainly result in a faster download.) Choose your version and download it, but don't unzip or install it yet!

GnuPG is a well-known security package, used by countless people all around the world. As such, if Mallory were to replace the official version of GnuPG with his own slightly modified version, he would have a back door into everyone's supposedly secure data. Therefore, the GnuPG software distribution is a target for all sorts of bad people, from bored teenagers to criminals.

You must be certain that the software you download is the same software that the GnuPG developers made available. (This is equally true of the PGP software, but PGP is provided by a corporation with a staff paid to take care of download integrity. Volunteers provide GnuPG.) That's where checksums come into play.

Checking Checksums

A *checksum* (related to a hash, as discussed in Chapter 1) is a "fingerprint" of a file. If the file changes in any way, the checksum also changes. Mathematicians have developed many different methods of generating checksums, but the GnuPG developers prefer the SHA1 method.

If you look at the download site closely, you'll see three offerings for any given version of GnuPG.

```
❶GnuPG 1.4.0a compiled for Microsoft Windows.
❷Signature and SHA-1 checksum for previous file.
❸28be01b7f8eaa29db73d11bf8b9504e823c07c2b
❹gnupg-w32cli-1.4.0a.zip
```

The first entry is ❶ the GnuPG program itself. The second entry is ❷ a file containing a digital signature of the first download. A download is a message like any other, and checking its digital signature is the preferred way to confirm its integrity. This gives us a chicken-and-egg problem, however: How can you verify the signature on the software that verifies signatures? Fortunately, you have an alternative. The developers have made a ❸ checksum available for the ❹ downloaded file gnupg-w32cli-1.4.0a.zip. (Remember, a checksum is similar to a hash.) Although a checksum alone isn't as reliable as a complete digital signature, it's better than nothing.

Calculating Checksums Under Windows

Microsoft operating systems do not include a checksum calculator, but there are many freely available. GnuPG makes a Windows checksum calculator freely available at www.gnupg .org, but it's not as full-featured as I would prefer. I like DigestIT 2004, a freeware program that integrates nicely into the Windows desktop. You can find DigestIT easily via a Google search or by following the link on www.pgp-gpg .com. When you right-click a file, a "digestIT 2004" menu item offers you the choice of calculating or comparing both MD5 and SHA1 checksums. Checksums are so valuable a tool for verifying the integrity of downloaded software that I highly recommend installing and conscientiously using this tool.

Calculating Checksums Under Unix

Many Unix-like operating systems (including any BSD and most versions of Linux) include a SHA1 checksum calculator. If one is not included, you can download it from your system vendor's website. Compute the checksum of a file simply by running the sha1 or sha1sum command, as follows. (If your system has neither sh1 or sha1sum, it probably has openssl. Use openssl sha1 instead.)

```
# sha1 gnupg-w32cli-1.4.0a.zip
SHA1 (gnupg-w32cli-1.4.0a.zip) = ❶28be01b7f8eaa29db73d11bf8b9504e823c07c2b
#
```

Compare ❶ the checksum generated by your checksum program to the checksum provided by the GnuPG developers.[1] If they match, you can be fairly certain that Mallory has not tampered with the software you downloaded.

NOTE *For the best possible security without using digital signatures, compare the checksum of the file with a checksum taken from a different download site.*

Regardless of how you calculate your checksums, if they do not match, your download was corrupted, your checksum program is defective, the GnuPG developers didn't update their checksum when they updated the software, or the software might have been tampered with on the original website. The most likely case is that your download went amok in some way. Try downloading again, perhaps from a different site. If you still cannot get a download with a matching checksum, ask for help on the gnupg-users mailing list (available at www.gnupg.org).

No matter which version of GnuPG you install, you'll have a GnuPG home directory with several important files. Although that directory won't exist until you install your desired version of GnuPG, we'll look at this common information before proceeding to platform-specific details.

GnuPG Home Directory

GnuPG stores all its information in a home directory. On Unix-like systems, this directory defaults to $HOME/.gnupg. On Microsoft operating systems, it defaults to C:\Documents and Settings*username*\Application Data\Gnu\GnuPG. We'll refer to this directory as the GnuPG home directory. Unless you have a really good reason to not use the default directory location (and enjoy typing additional command-line options every time you run a program), stick with the default.

GnuPG will create several files in this directory.

secring.gpg   Your secret keyring

pubring.gpg   Your public keyring

---

[1] Of course, in this example we're checking the Windows version on a Unix-like system, which isn't entirely useful. But you get the idea.

trustdb.gpg	Your trust database
gpg.conf	Your GnuPG configuration

The only one of these files that you need to be at all concerned with right now is gpg.conf (the rest of the files are discussed in Chapter 7). The gpg.conf file is where you store any local options for using GnuPG. (We'll discuss various options that you might set throughout the book.)

gpg.conf

If gpg.conf doesn't exist in your GnuPG home directory, go ahead and create it. (On a Windows system, be sure to use a text editor such as Notepad, not a word processor such as Microsoft Word.)

The gpg.conf file contains a number of variables, and each ❷ variable name is followed by its ❸ value. For example, here the variable *keyserver* is assigned the value hkp://subkeys.pgp.net.

```
#❶preferred keyserver
keyserver❷ hkp://subkeys.pgp.net❸
```

Lines in gpg.conf that begin with ❶ a hash mark (#) are comments.

Some variables have no value; their mere presence enables them. For example, adding the statement no-secmem-warning on its own line to gpg.conf silences those annoying "using insecure memory" messages that you see on some Unix-like systems.

NOTE *If you're using a Microsoft operating system, make sure that Windows doesn't automatically add an extension to the filenames when you edit, such as gpg.conf.txt. This will confuse GnuPG, which will in turn confuse you.*

Installing GnuPG on Windows

GnuPG runs on both Windows NT–based systems (including 2000, 2003, XP, and their descendants) as well as Windows 95–based systems (such as Windows Me and the various permutations of Windows 98).

If you are the only user of your system, installation is very simple, but there are very serious security concerns when using GnuPG on a multiuser Windows 95–based system. Remember, Windows 95 isn't really a multiuser operating system; the multiuser functions are an afterthought and really only amount to letting each user choose individual wallpaper and icons. Anyone with physical access to that system can get at your confidential data, and there's nothing you can do about it.

NOTE *No matter which version of GnuPG you install, you probably also want to add the gpg program to your PATH environment variable, so that you can run gpg from a command prompt. To do so, right-click **My Computer** and select **Properties**. Go to the **Advanced** tab and select the **Environment Variables** button. In the System Variables box, you'll see a PATH variable. Edit it to include the path to your completed GnuPG installation.*

Command-Line GnuPG Win32 Installation

At heart, GnuPG is a command-line program, which means that installing it won't be as pointy-clicky as, say, installing Microsoft Office. Most Windows users prefer a GUI client with nice buttons and boxes, however, and GnuPG has several. We'll discuss the freely available Windows Privacy Tray, or WinPT, in the next section. But first, here's how to install the command-line version of GnuPG on your machine.

NOTE *If you prefer a pointy-clicky GnuPG, skip to the next section and install WinPT instead of the command-line version.*

1. Go to www.gnupg.org and follow the Download link. You'll see a link for GnuPG for Windows. Download the software to a temporary location on your hard drive and double-click the EXE file to begin the installation.

2. GnuPG will start by asking you which language you want the installer to use, as shown in Figure 4-1. As of this writing, the GnuPG installer supports English and German, but more will be added as volunteers do the work. It will then show a very typical Welcome screen, display the GPL license for your perusal, and finally allow you to choose the components you need. A complete GnuPG version 1.4.2 install takes only 4.2 MB, so you may as well simply install the whole thing. (This is smaller than many video files people mail around today!)

Figure 4-1: Installer Language selection

3. You'll get a chance to choose the language GnuPG will use—not the installer language, as you were shown before, but the actual installed language. As shown in Figure 4-2, you can choose among many different tongues, from Belarusian to Turkish, including assorted variants of Chinese, Portuguese, Spanish, and other dialects of common languages.

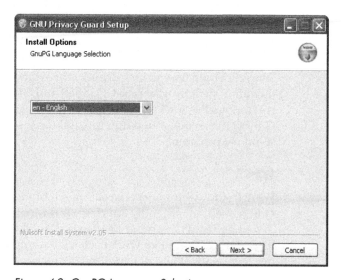

Figure 4-2: GnuPG Language Selection

4. Allow the installer to use the default folder, as shown in Figure 4-3—many add-on tools expect to find GnuPG there and will be easily confused by changes—and let it create the Start Menu item. When you click **Next** again, GnuPG will be installed on your machine and ready to go! After GnuPG is installed, you must create an OpenPGP keypair, as discussed at the end of this chapter. The key creation process is the same for both Windows and Unix-like versions of GnuPG.

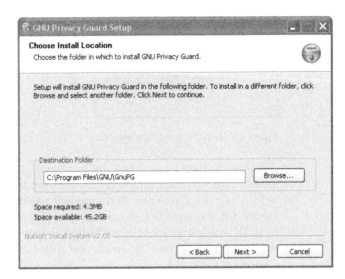

Figure 4-3: The GnuPG installation folder

Graphical GnuPG Installation

Several people have written GnuPG for Windows front ends,
including such programs as GPGShell and GPGEE. My favorite
is Windows Privacy Tray, or WinPT, a graphical interface for
GnuPG that is integrated into the desktop just like any other
Windows program.

WinPT

WinPT (www.winpt.org) conceals much of the complexity of
GnuPG behind a friendly interface. If you're just interested
in getting GnuPG working in a hurry, WinPT is for you. If you
find that you don't like WinPT, check out some of the alternative front ends. They all have similar functions, and when you
can work one, you can work them all.

NOTE *WinPT is integrated with a particular release of GnuPG, and
changes to GnuPG might make WinPT stop working; therefore, WinPT
includes the appropriate version in its install file. This means that you
shouldn't install the command-line version of GnuPG before installing
WinPT.*

To install WinPT:

1. First, create a WinPT folder in My Documents and set the
   permissions on the WinPT folder so that only you have
   the right to access it. As of this writing, the WinPT installer

does not allow you to create this folder during the install. (This might well be fixed by the time you read this; WinPT is improving rapidly.)

2. After you create the folder, run the installer by clicking the EXE file. The installer will display a warning about user rights, as shown in Figure 4-4. This warning only means that if you're not an administrative user of this machine, you won't have the permissions needed to install WinPT in the standard directory. You know you should be installing GnuPG only on a system that you control, but you might decide to do otherwise. GnuPG allows you to verify signatures even if you don't have your own private key, after all, and signature verification is an important tool in many environments.

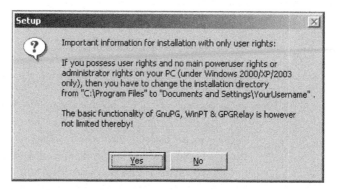

Figure 4-4: WinPT user rights message

3. You'll be presented with the typical Welcome to the GnuPT Setup Wizard – Close All Your Other Applications screen and click-through licenses. The license in this case is the GNU GPL, just like the GnuPG license itself.

4. When asked to choose the installation folder, use the default C:\Program Files\GnuPT folder if at all possible. Other people will be more able to help you use WinPT if you hold close to the standards.

5. Setup will ask you to choose a folder for your *keyrings*: the files containing your private key and any public keys you accumulate while using GnuPG. Use the WinPT folder you created under My Documents.

6. The Select Components screen (see Figure 4-5) allows you to choose which components of WinPT you want to install. WinPT includes three main programs: GnuPG itself (mandatory), Windows Privacy Tray, and GPGRelay.

GPGRelay works around problems with email client plug-ins, and is needed only for very specific situations. You almost certainly don't need it, and I recommend not installing it. Unselect the GPGRelay box and continue.

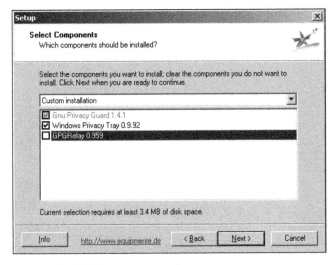

Figure 4-5: WinPT components selection

7. Several more screens offer the options to add desktop shortcuts, Start Menu options, and all the usual Windows bells and whistles. The Select Additional Tasks screen determines exactly how WinPT will integrate GnuPG with your system and allows you to choose which file types will be associated with WinPT and GnuPG. Take the defaults, letting WinPT handle .asc, .pgp, .gpg, and .sig files. Also keep the default to have WinPT start with Windows.

8. After you finish, the installer configures WinPT on your system as you specified. If you've never used GnuPG on this system, it will then complain that it cannot open your public and secret keyrings, as shown in Figure 4-6. This is normal—you haven't created them yet! Fortunately, it offers you more options if you just click **Yes**.

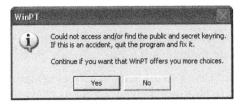

Figure 4-6: WinPT failing to find its keys

9. WinPT offers two options, as shown in Figure 4-7: Generate a new GnuPG keypair or copy a GnuPG key from another location. The latter option is useful if you are upgrading your WinPT install or migrating from another computer, but we're starting from scratch, so we want to generate a new keypair.

Figure 4-7: WinPT key options

Creating Keypairs in WinPT

WinPT displays the Key Generation Wizard, beginning with a screen that asks for your real name and email address. Strictly speaking, you can have an OpenPGP key that contains only a name and an email address, but after reading Chapter 2 you should know all sorts of things that your key should include. Note the **Expert** box in the lower-right corner, as shown in Figure 4-8. Because you're reading this book, WinPT will con-sider you an expert. Select it.

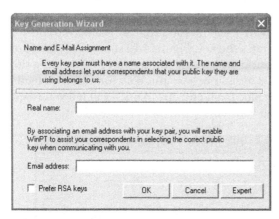

Figure 4-8: The basic WinPT key generator

The expert form is much more useful and detailed, allow-ing you to create keys with all the features we've discussed. Figure 4-9 shows the expert form.

We discussed the details of OpenPGP keys in Chapter 2, but here are a few reminders. Leave the Key Type and Subkey Size fields at their defaults, unless you have some reason for wanting a key with limited abilities or a very hard-to-break key. Use your real legal name as it appears on your identification if you want people to sign your key. The comment is free-form text to separate you from all the other people with your name. The email address should be an address that you control. Give the key an expiration date one year from the current date, and enter your chosen passphrase twice.

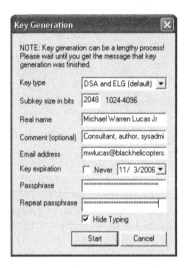

Figure 4-9: The expert WinPT key generator

WinPT will fill the Progress Dialog with plus signs (+) as it generates the key. Figure 4-10 shows a partially-completed key generation as it runs. If it seems to be running slowly, wiggle your mouse or browse the Web for awhile to feed your system some nice fresh entropy. WinPT will tell you when it has completed your keys.

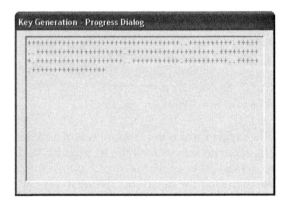

Figure 4-10: Key generation is proceeding.

Key Manager

After you complete your WinPT install, you'll see a magnifying glass icon in the system tray (the lower-right corner of the screen). This is the WinPT process. Double-click this icon to bring up the WinPT Key Manager: a simple GUI that lists each key in your keyring with menus to handle the most common GnuPG operations. The Key Manager should list the key you created during the install, along with lots of space to list other keys you'll accumulate, as shown in Figure 4-11.

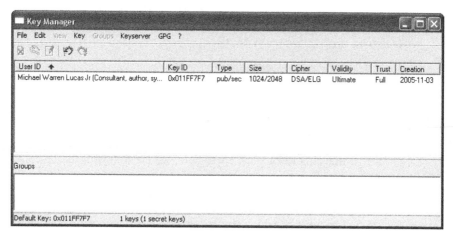

Figure 4-11: The WinPT Key Manager

Be sure to back up your key, including the private key. To do so, select your key in the Key Manager and choose **Key ▶ Export Secret Key**. You'll get a warning, stating that you shouldn't make this key public, and then WinPT will let you choose a place to store the backup file. Copy the secret key to a secure location, as discussed in Chapter 2.

WinPT Revocation Certificate

Next, create a revocation certificate with WinPT.

1. Open the Key Manager, right-click the key, and select **Revoke**. The pop-up window (shown in Figure 4-12) gives you everything you need to create a revocation certificate.

2. Although a revocation certificate can list a standard reason why the key is being revoked, in this case we don't know why—we only know that we want to have a revocation certificate on hand in case it becomes necessary. Select **No Reason Specified** in the first field.

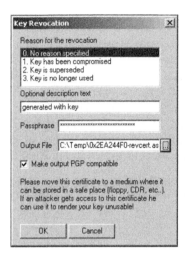

*Figure 4-12: WinPT revocation
certificate creation*

3. The description text is optional, but I find it useful to state that this revocation certificate was created with the key.

4. To access your private key, you must, of course, use your passphrase.

5. List a file in which the revocation certificate will be stored. Although WinPT uses a default filename of the keyid, you need to specify a directory to put the file in. Don't forget to put the revocation certificate in a safe place, perhaps with your backup of your secret key.

6. Leave the Make Output PGP Compatible box checked, so PGP users will recognize your revocation certificate.

Sending Your Key to a Keyserver

After you have a revocation certificate, you can publish your key to a keyserver. To do so, right-click your key, select **Send To Keyserver**, and choose one of the listed keyservers.

You can set a default keyserver in the Key Manager by selecting the Keyserver tab. The list of keyservers displayed here is stored in the file C:\Program Files\GnuPT\WPT\ keyserver.conf; if you have a different preferred keyserver, add it to this file and restart the Key Manager.

NOTE *If you're only using WinPT, and not the command-line GnuPG tools, you can skip the rest of this chapter and proceed directly to Chapter 5. The rest of us will take a look at GnuPG on a Unix-like system and then see how to create a key on the command line.*

Installing GnuPG on Unix-like Systems

If you don't want to build your own GnuPG binary from source, check the freeware and shareware download sites for your operating system. Volunteers maintain GnuPG for commercial operating systems such as AIX, Solaris, HP/UX, and so on. These packages are usually built with the operating system's native packaging tools, and you should read the documentation carefully.

Open-source, Unix-like operating systems such as Linux and BSD either include GnuPG out of the box or simplify GnuPG installation. You should confirm that the version of GnuPG included in your OS is recent, however, because some open-source operating systems are notoriously slow to update their included packages. Use gpg --version to print the installed program's version.

The two most common ways to install GnuPG are with RPMs under Linux systems such as Fedora Core and Red Hat, and the ports/packages system used by BSDs. To install GnuPG from an RPM, download the RPM and run the following:

```
# rpm --install gnupg-rpm-name.rpm
```

The BSDs place GnuPG's installation kit in either /usr/ports/security/gnupg (FreeBSD, OpenBSD) or /usr/pkgsrc/security/gnupg (NetBSD). Go to that directory and run the following to automatically build and install GnuPG configured appropriately for that OS:

```
# make all install clean
```

Those of you with more than a passing familiarity with RPM and/or BSD ports know of more features in your system's packaging tools (and there are also Debian's apt-get and Solaris' pkgadd). Feel free to use whatever tool is packaged with your OS to install GnuPG as packaged for that OS.

Randomness and GnuPG

GnuPG uses random numbers to produce keypairs and to encrypt messages. Although randomness is very easy to come by in the real world—just drop an egg and look at the splash—one of a computer's defining characteristics is its lack of randomness.

Computers are supposed to produce identical results every time they repeat an action. Although there are ways to generate truly random numbers on a computer, some operating systems don't use them and instead provide *pseudo-random* number generators. (Worse, some claim that their pseudo-random number generators are actually random!) Mallory has used these known pseudo-random numbers to break cryptographic keys. Using GnuPG successfully requires a reasonably excellent randomness source.

Although Windows, Linux, and BSDs provide good randomness, many commercial Unix-like operating systems do not, including even commercial systems such as AIX, HP/UX, and older Solaris. Some of these systems have randomness-generating add-ons, or experienced sysadmins have some trick that can be used to provide randomness, but these methods might or might not be standards-compliant and might not work with GnuPG.

Entropy Gathering Daemon

The Entropy Gathering Daemon, or EGD, was written to provide randomness for GnuPG. EGD is a Perl script that runs various system programs that produce unpredictable output (such as top, vmstat, and so on) and scrambles it all together into an acceptable randomness source. You must have Perl 5.004 or greater installed to use EGD.

EGD is not as good a randomness source as the ones available in other operating systems, but it's sufficient for a GnuPG user to feel reasonably secure. Windows, Linux, and BSD do not require EGD. You can download EGD from the GnuPG website or a mirror. After you download it, verify the checksum of the downloaded package and extract it. To install EGD, follow these steps:

1. Change to the directory where you extracted the files and run the following:

    ```
    # perl Makefile.pl
    # make test
    # make install
    #
    ```

    You will find egd.pl in either /usr/bin or /usr/local/bin, depending on your Perl configuration.

2. If you've never run GnuPG on this particular computer before, create a .gnupg directory in your home account.

3. EGD defaults to providing randomness in the file .gnupg/entropy, but it cannot create that directory itself. To create the directory, start EGD a few moments before running

GnuPG (or, better still, before even installing GnuPG—the build process creates a decent chunk of entropy).

```
# egd.pl ~/.gnupg/entropy
#
```

4. You must inform GnuPG when you use EGD instead of the system's (nonexistent) randomness-providing device. To do so, add the following line to your gpg.conf file:

```
load-extension rndegd
```

Or, add the command-line argument --load-extension=rndegd whenever you run GnuPG. (Personally, I don't care to remember or type any more command-line options than I strictly must!)

Building from Source Code

Your access to source code is the whole purpose of GnuPG's license. If you're a computer user who just wants your programs to work and you don't care about how to actually build the software from source code, you probably want to skip to the next section now. Those of you who use make like other people use Solitaire can continue.

GnuPG began as a Unix-only program, and its source code shows it. In fact, the Windows version of GnuPG distributed by the GnuPG project is actually cross-compiled on a Unix-like system.

NOTE *Although you can build GnuPG on a Windows system, you need a fairly high level of skill to do so. We'll assume that you're building in the GnuPG native Unix-like environment.*

Installing GnuPG

GnuPG is usually built with the Gnu C compiler (GCC), gmake, and autoconf, which are all freely available in any number of places on the Internet. If you don't have them installed on your system, you'll need to get them before you can build GnuPG. See the documentation for these programs separately to install them correctly. After you have these programs, follow these steps:

1. Download the GnuPG source code from the website or a mirror. Verify the checksum to confirm that you have good source code.

2. The GnuPG source is distributed as a bzipped tarball, so uncompress and extract it:

```
# bunzip gnupg-1.4.0.tar.bz2 | tar -xf -
```

The resulting directory contains several text files of information and the files necessary to build the software. Some interesting files include README, which contains a brief introduction to GnuPG, and INSTALL, which gives detailed instructions on how to build GnuPG from source code and get it running on your system.

3. The configure script checks your system to see if you have everything ready to actually compile GnuPG. For a stock GnuPG setup, just run the following:

```
# ./configure
```

Configuration Options

Most of the user-configurable changes provided by GnuPG can be set by command-line options at the configure step. For a list of possible configure options, you can use the --help option. For your convenience, however, here are a couple of popular options:

- If you need to use EGD to provide randomness on your particular operating system, you can tell GnuPG about it with the --enable-static-rnd=egd option. This option eliminates any need for configuration file settings or command-line options to tell GnuPG you're using EGD.

- The --prefix option allows you to choose where to place the completed programs and documents.

For example, to build your own version of GnuPG that requires the EGD and installs the binaries under your account, run the following:

```
# ./configure --enable-static-rnd=egd --prefix=/home/mwlucas
```

If your system has everything you need to build GnuPG, the configure process will spew several screens of information and return you to a command prompt without complaining. However, if your system cannot build GnuPG for some reason, the configure script will issue warnings and terminate early. Those errors must be fixed before you can continue!

After you configure GnuPG, build and install it:

```
# make
# make install
#
```

If you have a problem building GnuPG, you're probably not the first one who has had your exact problem. First, read the failure and see if you understand it. If you don't, check Google and the gnupg-users mailing list archive (available from www.gnupg.org) for other appearances of the same error message. If neither of these provides an answer, ask the question on the gnupg-users mailing list.

Setuid Root GnuPG

Whenever you start GnuPG on a Unix-like system, you might see a message like this:

```
gpg: WARNING: using insecure memory!
gpg: please see http://www.gnupg.org/faq.html for more information
```

Operating systems have a feature called *virtual memory*, in which the less-frequently used contents of the system memory are written to disk to make memory space for programs that are more active. GnuPG is complaining that it's using more memory than the operating system could write to disk, possibly allowing another system user who has superb[2] systems knowledge to access your private key. This is definitely a problem.

To make this problem go away, allow the program gpg to run as root by turning on the setuid bit. Setuid programs cannot have memory they use written to disk. These programs have a bad reputation in the security world because they have been used to break into more than one server. For this reason, GnuPG doesn't install itself as a setuid root program. Each systems administrator should decide whether he wants to add another setuid program to the system.

---

[2] Those people who know how to do this will probably tell me it's easy. I'm sure it is after you do it once. Just like running a marathon or bowling a perfect game.

In the case of GnuPG, using setuid root makes a lot of sense. To change your installed GnuPG program to be setuid root, run the following:

```
# chown root /usr/local/bin/gpg*
# chgrp wheel /usr/local/bin/gpg*
# chmod 4755 /usr/local/bin/gpg*
```

If you don't have privilege to do this on your system, talk to your systems administrator. (And stop using GnuPG on a system you don't control!)

If you don't want to install gpg as a setuid root program, you can at least silence the warning by adding the option no-secmem-warning to your gpg.conf file. It doesn't eliminate the "memory writing to disk problem," but at least GnuPG will stop rubbing your nose in it.

Don't Run GnuPG as Root

Now that you have your GnuPG program installed exactly as you like, let's use this beastie. Although you must be root to install GnuPG on your system, you should not be root when running GnuPG. The root account is reserved for system administration and problem resolution and should not be used for day-to-day work.

NOTE *Those of you whose systems display a hash mark (#) for a root-level command prompt should not be confused by the presence of a hash mark as a prompt in the examples in this book. GnuPG is designed to be used by a unique regular user in everyday work, not by the root account. (And stop relying on the prompt to tell you whether you are root or not; Mallory can muck with your prompt with only minimal difficulty!)*

Command-Line GnuPG Keypairs

As with any other OpenPGP implementation, you must create a keypair before you can use most of GnuPG's functions. Remember, generate your keys only on a machine that you control. If you leave your keypair lying around for anyone to use, that anyone can pretend to be you! (By the way, the keypairs used in these examples are not my real OpenPGP key. You can find my real keyid and fingerprint on a variety of keyservers.)

You might be using command-line GnuPG on either Unix-like or Windows systems. Both have command prompts that look very different, but the GnuPG functions are identical. I will use a Unix-style hash mark as a command prompt, if for no other reason than because it's shorter than the Windows-style C:>Program Files\ prompt. Open whichever sort of command prompt you have and follow along.

Create your OpenPGP keypair by entering the following:

```
# gpg --gen-key❶
gpg (GnuPG) 1.4.0; Copyright (C) 2004 Free Software Foundation, Inc.
This program comes with ❷ABSOLUTELY NO WARRANTY.
This is free software, and you are welcome to redistribute it
under certain conditions. See the file COPYING for details.

gpg: please see http://www.gnupg.org/faq.html for more information
gpg: keyring `/home/mwlucas/.gnupg/secring.gpg' created❸
gpg: keyring `/home/mwlucas/.gnupg/pubring.gpg' created❹
```

The ❶ --gen-key option tells GnuPG to create a new keypair. Every time you start GnuPG, it reminds you of its ❷ warranty (none) and its licensing terms (GPL). The first time you run GnuPG, the program creates a directory to store your ❸ private keys, your ❹ public keys, and other GnuPG information. We'll look at these files in more detail throughout the next few chapters.

```
Please select what kind of key you want:
   (1) DSA and Elgamal (default)
   (2) DSA (sign only)
   (5) RSA (sign only)
Your selection? 5❶
```

While the default key generation method has been used for several years, it is beginning to show its age. Choose ❶ an RSA key instead.

```
RSA keys may be between 1024 and 4096 bits long.
What keysize do you want? (2048) 2048
Requested keysize is 2048 bits
```

GnuPG uses a default key size of 2048 bits, which will provide robust security for the next several years unless your attacker has quantum computers or one of those ultra-secret, custom-built code-busting machines the NSA is rumored to have.

As I mentioned earlier, increasing the key size increases the amount of work needed to process your key. Remember that unless you know that the person you're sending the message to has sufficient computing power to decrypt the message, stick with the defaults here.

Once you choose a keysize, GnuPG will ask for the expiration date of this key.

```
Requested keysize is 2048 bits
Please specify how long the key should be valid.
         0 = key does not expire
      <n>  = key expires in n days
      <n>w = key expires in n weeks
      <n>m = key expires in n months
      <n>y = key expires in n years
Key is valid for? (0) 1y
Key expires in 1 year
Is this correct? (y/N) y
```

We discussed expiration times in Chapter 2. Having your first key last for a year is a sensible choice; a non-expiring key might seem simpler, but only stores up future problems.

Now assign a name and email address to your key:

```
You need a user ID to identify your key; the software constructs the user ID
from the Real Name, Comment and Email Address in this form:
    "Heinrich Heine (Der Dichter) <heinrichh@duesseldorf.de>"

Real name: Michael Warren Lucas Jr❶
Email address: mwlucas@blackhelicopters.org❷
Comment: Author, consultant, sysadmin❸
```

When you enter information here, give ❶ your legal, real name as it appears on government documents (for reasons we discussed in Chapter 2), as well as ❷ your email address and ❸ a comment to differentiate you from all the other people in the world who have your name. GnuPG responds with the following:

```
You selected this USER-ID:
    "Michael Warren Lucas Jr (Author, consultant, sysadmin) <mwlucas@
blackhelicopters.org>"
Change (N)ame, (C)omment, (E)mail or (O)kay/(Q)uit? o
```

You'd feel rather daft if you generated a key and got it signed by a whole slew of people, only to discover that you'd made a typo. This is your chance to double-check your work and make sure that everything is spelled correctly and that you have used the desired values. You can change any entry by choosing the appropriate option or just enter **o** to continue.

After you confirm your identity information, GnuPG will let you select a passphrase:

```
You need a Passphrase to protect your secret key.

Enter passphrase:
```

Remember from Chapter 1 that a passphrase is like a password, but can be much longer. This passphrase protects your secret key so that only you can use it. Make your passphrase something that you can remember without too much trouble but will be difficult for other people to guess. GnuPG prompts for your passphrase twice and complains if your entries differ, just as if you were changing your password in most other programs.

And now this:

```
We need to generate a lot of random bytes. It is a good idea to perform
some other action (type on the keyboard, move the mouse, utilize the
disks) during the prime generation; this gives the random number
generator a better chance to gain enough entropy.
..+++++.+++++++++++++++++++++++++++++++++++++++..+++++++++++++++++h+++++++u.++++
...
```

Your operating system provides randomness on demand, either via its built-in randomness facilities or through an add-on such as EGD. This randomness comes from actions that the computer cannot control, such as when the mouse is moved or when network packets arrive.

At times, your computer can run short of random numbers and might need your help creating some more. If the key-generation process takes more than a few seconds, wiggle your mouse, open up a web page, or type a document while leaving your command prompt running in the background. (Wiggling a mouse is generally agreed to be an excellent randomness source if your operating system supports it. Windows does; Linux and BSD might, depending on the version you're using; and most commercial Unix-like operating systems don't.) Shortly, GnuPG will spit out confirmation of your new keypair:

```
gpg: /home/mwlucas/.gnupg/trustdb.gpg: trustdb created
gpg: key D4ED7B9F❶ marked as ultimately trusted❷
public and secret key created and signed.❸
```

```
gpg: checking the trustdb
gpg: 3 marginal(s) needed, 1 complete(s) needed, PGP trust model
gpg: depth: 0 valid:   1 signed:   0 trust: 0-, 0q, 0n, 0m, 0f, 1u
pub   1024D/D4ED7B9F 2007-02-10
      Key fingerprint = 9F53 C982 D561 3506 95B5  5C82 7EC4 29B8 D4ED 7B9F❹
uid          Michael Warren Lucas Jr (Author, consultant, sysadmin) <mwlucas@
blackhelicopters.org>
sub   2048g/A3D15F1E 2007-02-10
#
```

Here you learn about your key. First, the key is known by a keyid, or "shorthand name" of ❶ D4ED7B9F. Although this keyid is not unique among the worldwide pool of OpenPGP users, it helps to easily differentiate among keys on your private keyring. You ❷ completely trust this key—it's been generated on the local machine, and if you can't trust yourself then you have problems that GnuPG can't help you with. You also see that ❸ both the public and secret keys have been created and signed.

The ❹ key fingerprint is a human-readable method of identifying a public key. This is not absolutely guaranteed to be unique—like hashes, it's just barely possible that someone else, someone in the world, had the extreme fortune to have a matching key fingerprint, much as it is just barely possible that you could be killed by a meteorite. When combined with your name and email address, though, the fingerprint is certainly unique.

GnuPG Revocation Certificates

Generating a revocation certificate requires that you have access to your private key, know your passphrase, and have a compatible version of an OpenPGP-compliant system. The easiest way to guarantee this is to generate your revocation certificate as soon as you have created your keypair! To do so, run the following on a command line:

```
# gpg -a --output mwlucas@blackhelicopters.org.asc.revoke❶ --gen-revoke❷
mwlucas@blackhelicopters.org❸
```

Here, we tell GnuPG to put its output in a file called ❶ mwlucas@blackhelicopters.org.asc.revoke. (I store revocation certificates in a file named after the email account they're associated with, but if you have a better system feel free to use it.)

We tell GnuPG to ❷ generate a revocation certificate for the UID containing ❸ mwlucas@blackhelicopters.org. GnuPG will first print out the key information and then give you a chance to confirm that you want to create a revocation certificate for this key.

```
sec  1024D/D4ED7B9F 2007-02-10 Michael Warren Lucas Jr (Author, consultant,
sysadmin) <mwlucas@blackhelicopters.org>
Create a revocation certificate for this key? (y/N) y
Please select the reason for the revocation:
  0 = No reason specified
  1 = Key has been compromised
  2 = Key is superseded
  3 = Key is no longer used
  Q = Cancel
(Probably you want to select 1 here)
Your decision? 0❶
```

Because you've just generated this key and have no idea why you might eventually want to revoke it, enter ❶ a 0 here. The reason for revoking the key is not as important as the fact that it has been revoked, and the revocation certificate will be respected without a reason.

```
Enter an optional description; end it with an empty line:
> Revocation certificate generated when key created❶
> ❷
Reason for revocation: No reason specified
Revocation certificate generated when key created
Is this okay? (y/N) y❸
```

GnuPG will ask for ❶ a reason for revoking the key (it doesn't need to be long). End your description with ❷ a single empty line, and say ❸ yes when prompted.

```
You need a passphrase to unlock the secret key for
user: "Michael Warren Lucas Jr (Author, consultant, sysadmin) <mwlucas@
blackhelicopters.org>"
1024-bit DSA key, ID D4ED7B9F, created 2007-02-10

Enter passphrase:
```

After you enter your passphrase to unlock your private key, GnuPG will create the revocation certificate in the file you specified and spit out a brief message about how to handle and secure your key and revocation certificate.

Publicizing Your Key

If you use PGP, the software automatically publicizes your key in the PGP Global Directory (aka "The PGP Corporation's Keyserver"). As a GnuPG user, you can choose any key publicizing method from "don't publicize" to "broadcast to the world." The standard ways include posting on a web page or other Internet medium (finger, ftp, and so on), or exporting to a keyserver. We'll look at both.

Text Exports

While your public key is stored in the file pubring.gpg in your GnuPG home directory, don't just put this file out on your web page! It also contains all the other public keys you've added to your keyring. OpenPGP defines a standard method for presenting public keys in text, so that web browsers can display them easily. GnuPG provides tools to extract your public key from your keyring in a format that is most useful to others.

Unlike extracting a real key from a physical keyring, extracting your public key from your keyring simply copies the key into another file.

```
# gpg --output pubkey.mwlucas@blackhelicopters.org.gpg❶ --export mwlucas❷
```

Here, we use GnuPG to create a file, ❶ pubkey.mwlucas@ blackhelicopters.org.gpg, which contains our public key. We tell GnuPG which key to export by using ❷ part of the UID. If my public keyring contained more than one key with the string "mwlucas" in it, I'd need to use a more complete description of the key.

If you look at the the public key's file we just created, you'll see nothing but computer-readable binary data (also known as "garbage"). Binary data is great for machines, but lousy for email, web pages, or other human-friendly systems. To make your public key more friendly to the eye, you can convert it to ASCII characters with the --armor[3] option:

```
# gpg --output pubkey.mwlucas@blackhelicopters.org.gpg.asc  --armor ❶
--export mwlucas
```

---

[3] Different operating systems handle binary data differently, and email systems can damage binary data. *Armoring* binary data protects it by encoding it in old-fashioned ASCII. The fact that the armored data is human-readable is only a (beneficial) side effect.

The only difference between this command and the previous one is the addition of the ❶ --armor option. But the file we get is human-readable, and looks something like this:

```
-----BEGIN PGP PUBLIC KEY BLOCK-----
Version: GnuPG v1.4.0 (FreeBSD)

mQGiBEIL3skRBADyThL7faGX/JL7xZYL6TPYJzvxn5qHUTAO9Hw4o99OLTLMI7J3
14g6i7XTS37C9OntI8hAFZV7yaXXj5dA5pduIkuEVAmxat4OydPqqE31XNScIAnq
...
```

After a few dozen lines of these characters, you'll see a line like this one:

```
-----END PGP PUBLIC KEY BLOCK-----
```

There's your public key, in human-readable form. Of course, human-readable is obviously a very loose term; although you *can* read this, it doesn't mean you'd *want* to. Still, it's a lot easier on the eyes than the binary data. You can post this file on your website, or just copy and paste the text into your page. People hunting for your public key on your web page would prefer that you make your public key a downloadable file, however; it's much easier to import.

Keyservers

Before submitting your public key to a keyserver, you need to pick a keyserver. The list of keyservers changes frequently, so I won't provide a "top ten" list here; instead, I recommend that you use subkeys.pgp.net or just Google for a list of OpenPGP keyservers.

If you like to type, you can specify the keyserver on the GnuPG command line with the --keyserver option:

```
# gpg --keyserver❶ subkeys.pgp.net❷ --send-keys❸ mwlucas@blackhelicopters
.org❹
gpg: success sending to 'subkeys.pgp.net'❺ (status=200)
#
```

Here we ❸ transmit the public key tied to our ❹ email address to ❶ the keyserver ❷ subkeys.pgp.net. The keyserver ❺ replies that it has received the key. Our public key will be globally visible to anyone who searches for it in the global keyserver pool very shortly, as soon as the keyservers have time to replicate their information among themselves.

The downside of the command-line option is that you must include it every time you communicate with a keyserver. This gets old quick.

To set a default keyserver in the gpg.conf file in the GnuPG home directory, set the keyserver option.

```
keyserver x-hkp://subkeys.pgp.net
```

If you must use a different keyserver while you have this set, setting a keyserver on the command line will override the setting in gpg.conf.

Web Forms

Some users report difficulty in contacting a keyserver from their network. I've never experienced this problem myself, but it's been reported in enough places that I'm perfectly willing to believe that some network designs don't play well with keyservers. If you have problems contacting a keyserver, try a web-based OpenPGP key submission method. If you browse to http://subkeys.pgp.net, you will probably find a web-based submission form somewhere on the site. If you don't, refresh the page again. Copy your ASCII public key and paste it into the submission form. This process should work even with minimal Internet access.

5

THE WEB OF TRUST

Now that you have your own personal keypair and have publicized your public key, you're ready to read any encrypted messages intended for you, and other people can verify that messages you send are actually from you. That's only half the process of confidential communication, however; you also need to be able to send people messages that only they can read and you need to be able to verify that messages from other people are actually from them. These tasks require other people's public keys. Public keys allow you to build your own personal Web of Trust and verify the identity of any OpenPGP user.

To begin, you must be comfortable getting other people's public keys from online sources such as keyservers.

Keyservers

Keyservers store OpenPGP public keys for general public access. If you followed the instructions during the OpenPGP install process, your public key should now be available on the keyservers subkeys.pgp.net and keyserver.pgp.com, and people should have no trouble finding it.

subkeys.pgp.net

The keyserver subkeys.pgp.net is an old-style PGP keyserver, from a time when only the technically elite used PGP (or the Internet, for that matter). It's actually several keyservers run by volunteers from all over the world, and each time you contact this machine, you're actually reaching a different server. After you upload a public key to any of these keyservers, it should be replicated and available on all of them within hours.

In the case of these servers, and unlike the keyserver hosted by PGP Corporation, anyone can upload any key to this keyserver. Old keys are never removed, and no verification of key ownership takes place when keys are uploaded. This means that if you're looking for an older key, you can find it on this server. It also means that people can upload test, bogus, or otherwise invalid keys to this keyserver, and these keys will remain there forever. (It should be obvious, but just in case: Do not submit test keys to keyservers! It is rude and annoying, and like discarded plastic bottles, test keys litter the landscape forever.)

If you're using GnuPG, I recommend subkeys.pgp.net as a default (unless you're lucky enough to have a more local keyserver mirror, such as those available at some universities). PGP can add subkeys.pgp.net to its keyserver list to check it automatically.

keyserver.pgp.com

The PGP Corporation provides keyserver.pgp.com as a public service, but it works differently from subkeys.pgp.net. Whenever anyone uploads a key to keyserver.pgp.com, the server sends an email to the address embedded in the key to confirm that the key legitimately belongs to that account. When the email recipient visits the link in the email, the key is made available on the keyserver.

Additionally, unlike subkeys.pgp.net, keys posted to keyserver.pgp.com that are unused for a period of time (six months as of this writing) are purged from the records. This has the effect of providing an up-to-date keyserver, but it isn't entirely compatible with the expectations of the older Open-PGP world.

The weak point of this model is that the PGP software assumes that the keys accepted by keyserver.pgp.com are valid. There is a certain safety in this assumption: To register a key, you must have access to the email address, but anyone can open an email address at a free provider and claim any legal name they like, however,[1] so this doesn't guarantee identity.

NOTE *PGP automatically checks for keys on keyserver.pgp.com, but GnuPG users must check for these keys manually (or set keyserver.pgp.com as their default keyserver).*

Searching for Keys

If your mail client doesn't automatically fetch the public key of OpenPGP-encrypted messages, you'll need to search the keyservers. Both GnuPG and OpenPGP can search keyservers for keys that match particular conditions.

Also, most keyservers have web interfaces. For example, to search for keys on keyserver.pgp.com, just call up the server in a web browser, enter the email address of the person whose key you want, and the web interface will let you download the key if it's on that keyserver.

The web interface for subkeys.pgp.net is more erratic. Because these servers are run by different volunteers, the website looks different between visits. You may find an introductory page in front of the keyserver query form, but the link to go to the keyserver page should be pretty obvious. If you don't like the particular keyserver page where you wind up, exit your browser and start over; you'll hit another server.

After you download the key and add it to your keyring, you can exchange private messages with that person. You can also attach yourself to the Web of Trust by signing keys and having your keys signed.

Signing a Key

By signing another person's key, you are affirming that you have verified that person's identity. This is called *trust* in the OpenPGP world. Remember, trust in the PGP sense means only that you trust the person's identity, not their trustworthiness as a person. Perhaps you went to school with the local car thief and know exactly who he is. You could sign his key

---

[1] "Of *course* the President has a Gmail account for personal stuff! The whitehouse.gov address looks so stuffy, don't you know. Now, about your credit card numbers . . . "

without a qualm because you can trust that he is who he says he is. You cannot trust him with your wallet or your pets, but you can trust his identity, and that's all that OpenPGP cares about.

To sign someone's key, the key owner must provide the prospective signer with the following:

- Her public key fingerprint, keyid, and user ID (UID) delivered via anything but the Internet
- Her public key (on a keyserver, web page, floppy disk, or similar source)
- Her email address
- Her full name
- Proof of her identity

Each key has a unique fingerprint and a keyid that is unique when combined with the UID. Both GnuPG and PGP will show you the fingerprint and keyid if you ask (you'll see how exactly in the following chapters). For instance, my example key has a fingerprint of 9F53 C982 D561 3506 95B5 5C82 7EC4 29B8 D4ED 7B9F and a keyid of D4ED7B9F. (The astute among you might notice that the keyid is simply the last eight characters of the fingerprint.) Every keypair has a similar-looking keyid and fingerprint.

The keyid and fingerprint must be delivered by any means other than the Internet. This seems to be an unnecessary hassle, but think about it. If a bad guy has hacked into your friend's email account, how can you trust that the fingerprint you receive from his email account is accurate? The same applies to fingerprints made available on his web page. You must receive the key through some offline mechanism.

After you have the fingerprint and UID, you can find the public key easily enough on keyservers.

The requirements for proof of identity will vary from person to person, depending on your relationship to that person. Let's look at a couple of examples.

Signing Keys of Friends and Family

Perhaps the easiest way to grow your keyring is through coworkers, friends, and relatives who use OpenPGP. I even use OpenPGP within my family—if I'm sending my wife private information, I encrypt it before sending. When I send security-related information to coworkers, I protect it with OpenPGP, so those coworkers need an OpenPGP-compliant program to read it.

Let's assume that a hypothetical new employee (we'll call him Matt) has just generated his keypair and needs me to sign it. I also want him to sign my keypair; not only will this expand his Web of Trust but to sign my key he must also add my key to his keyring. This means that he will be able to verify email that I send him. Matt produces a piece of paper with his keyid and fingerprint, and informs me that his public key is on a keyserver. He also has two pieces of government-issued ID.

Now, I know Matt. I hired him. I've already done a certain amount of identity verification on him by doing a background check, filing paperwork with the state, and so on. If he's attempting to deceive me about his identity, he's doing it with far more depth than I (or most people) can possibly penetrate.

First, I examine the photo ID to confirm that his name matches the name on the key. Although you probably wouldn't require government-issued ID to trust the identity of a coworker or friend, it is still smart to pay close attention to the form of the name used on the keypair. If Matt's driver's license shows his name as Matthew Peter Smith, but he created a key as Matt Smith, he might have trouble using the key later, depending on other people's signing standards. I insist that all keys used for work have names that match the correct legal identity—as the boss, that's my right. With a friend, I'll just point out the discrepancy and let him decide. In this case, as Matt's generated key doesn't match his legal identity; hence doesn't meet my signing requirements, and I won't sign it. (He'll probably wander off, muttering under his breath something about working for a hardcase nut job, but that's OK. The sooner he understands that I *am* a hardcase nut job, the better off he'll be.) If his UID matches his legal name and email address, and his keyid and fingerprint match those he gave me separately, I'll accept that this identity goes with this key.

After I have confirmed his identity, I'll download his key, sign it, and return it.

Signing Strangers' Keys

If you truly don't know someone at all—that is, if they are a true stranger—do not sign their key. But if I meet a client or prospective client who happens to use OpenPGP, I'll offer to verify and sign his key for him. When I meet the manager of an IT department at his office, I'm pretty sure that he is who he claims to be. Even if neither of us has a computer at hand, I can gather the information I need to sign his key and sign the key at my convenience.

First, I check his ID. This person should have two forms of ID with his full legal name on them. I prefer a driver's license and passport, but when someone doesn't have a passport I'll settle for student ID cards, organization memberships, and the like. I also check to see whether the ID is obviously forged. (Although I can't detect even a fair-to-middling forgery, I have seen a couple of drivers' licenses so badly forged that even I rejected them.) After I'm convinced that the ID is legitimate, I get the person's keyid, fingerprint, keyserver, and email address.

After I return to my computer, I'll download the person's key from the keyserver and compare these:

- The name in the UID to the person's legal name

- The email address in the UID to the person's stated email address

- The fingerprint of the key to the person's professed key

If they all match, then—and only then—will I sign the key.

NOTE *If you're willing to verify the identity and sign strangers' keys, you might check out OpenPGP social networking sites such as www .biglumber.com. These sites coordinate meetings between OpenPGP users in cities around the world. You can enter your key into the Big Lumber site, along with your name and city, and search for other OpenPGP users within the same city or nearby. It's fairly easy to contact these people and meet at a local coffee shop for five minutes to verify identity and exchange fingerprints.*

What to Do with Signed Keys

So you've signed a key; now what? Just as you learned as a child, after you're done with the key, put it back where you found it. If you downloaded the key from a public keyserver, you can update the record on that keyserver. If you got the key elsewhere, return the signed key to the key owner.

NOTE *You can send someone else's public key to an old-style keyserver. Although you might think this would be a favor, it's actually extremely rude. The public key owner might have reasons for not using a keyserver and might prefer to distribute his public key via some other method—or he might not want to publicize the key at all beyond a small group of people. Never publicize someone else's key for them!*

When You Get New Signatures

So, you've verified your identity to someone, and that person sent you a new public key file. How do you get that new signature onto your public key? This is simplicity itself. Just import the public key file into your own public keyring. Your software will figure out that it's your own key, sort out the new signatures, and add them to your ring. We will discuss importing keys with PGP in Chapter 6 and GnuPG in Chapter 7.

Keysigning Parties

The fastest way to accumulate signatures on your public key is to attend a keysigning party, which is a gathering of people for the specific purpose of verifying each other's identities and signing OpenPGP public keys. You don't have to know these people to have them sign your key, but you never know who knows who and what friends and acquaintances you might have in common. You might be asked to provide your keyid, fingerprint, and UID to the host ahead of time, or to bring several copies of it with you. (I recommend printing your UID and fingerprint multiple times on a sheet of paper and cutting the paper into multiple cards or strips so that you can distribute this information yourself, no matter what problems the host has.) Bring your photo ID, but do not bring a computer. Bring at least one copy of your UID and fingerprint with you, so that you can compare the copies other people have to your original.

Keysigning parties flow in a variety of ways, but the general method is that each person identifies himself to every other person in the room. If you've provided your key information to the host ahead of time, he will frequently give each person in the room a list of keys to be verified and signed. Otherwise, you'll need to give each person a written copy of your key information.

After everyone has the information on all the keys to be signed, people will take turns reading their own copy of their key fingerprint and UID to the attendees. (You might be asked to write your key information on an overhead projector instead, or otherwise broadcast your fingerprint.) This confirms that the party host didn't mix up key fingerprints when preparing the key lists and ensures that even if Mallory is hosting the keysigning party he can do very little damage.

When other people present their key information and ID, check them carefully just as if you were signing any other stranger's key. After you are satisfied with the owner's identity, mark a check next to that key on your list. If something about the owner or the key doesn't feel right to you, cross that key off the list. This is a situation in which you should listen to your gut—if you have any doubt whatsoever about the key's validity, cross it off your list!

After the party, but within the next day or two, get out your list of keys. Download those keys from the keyservers and compare them with the checked ones on your list. If you are satisfied that those keys you downloaded have the same finger-print as the fingerprints you checked at the keysigning party, and if the UID on the downloaded key matches the information you got at the keysigning party, sign the key and return it to the owner or the keyserver.

Key Trust

The word *trust* has many different meanings in OpenPGP, but when we speak of the trust we have in a key signer, we're concerned with how well the person verifies the identity of other OpenPGP users. Each public key you add to your keyring and sign needs to have one of three levels of trust assigned to it. The method for assigning trust varies with the OpenPGP program you're using, and is discussed in either Chapter 6 or Chapter 7.

None

Although I have verified the identity of the key owner, I do not trust this person's ability to verify the identity of other people's keys. You might use this trust level for family members or people who are obviously far too trusting.

Marginal

I have verified the identity of this key owner, and this person seems to be reasonably competent at verifying the identity of others. You might use this trust level for people you don't know, but who you meet at a keysigning party. If they've bothered to show up for a keysigning party, at least they know how things *should* work!

Trusted

I trust this person completely when it comes to verifying the identity of people and signing their OpenPGP keys.

You'll also see a fourth level of trust: implicit. This is reserved for keys that you also have the private key for. If you can use a key, chances are that you trust that key signer com-pletely—they're you, after all!

You'll see how to assign trust to keys as we import and sign them in both PGP and GnuPG.

Avoiding the Web of Trust

Using of the Web of Trust is not necessary for using OpenPGP. In fact, some users will not want to sign keys or participate in the Web of Trust at all. The Web of Trust shows everyone in the world a list of people you have met, after all. If someone investigates you, signatures on your OpenPGP key will provide a ready-made list of associates who should also be investigated. The "network profiling" investigatory technique involves identifying a hub of activity and drawing lines between this hub and other groups to identify other hubs. The CIA uses this for tracking terrorist cells, the DEA uses it to analyze drug trafficking, and the casino industry uses it to identify complex fraud schemes. The Web of Trust can assist network profilers.

For example, my wife and I have pet rats. We communicate with other pet rat owners to discuss health, breeding, training, and exchange photos of our four-footed families. We might use OpenPGP to retain message confidentiality. One day, though, the government might announce a "War on Rats." As a public rat-friendly figure, I would come under suspicion as a possible hub of ratty activity. The government can then use my OpenPGP keyring as a starting place to build its list of other suspects and watch for traffic between us rat-pushing fiends. If you don't want to be on the list of suspects, having me sign your key is not your wisest move. Likewise, I don't want to be investigated when your hobby is declared illegal, immoral, or fattening.

A safer method of key management is for you to personally verify the keys of people you must communicate with. You can make local (or non-exportable) signatures on those keys so that the signatures remain only on your local keyring and are not distributed to keyservers. This gives you all the advantages of OpenPGP, at the cost of personally verifying each key. Personal verification is still the best way to verify identity, anyway.

For the rest of this book, we'll assume that you will participate in the Web of Trust. Remember that you have a choice, however. Everyone's threat model differs, and only you know the risks you run.

6

PGP KEY MANAGEMENT

Managing OpenPGP keys with PGP is as simple as can be. After you configure your client, tasks such as finding and signing keys should take only seconds.

Adding Keyservers

PGP defaults to using the keyserver provided by the PGP Corporation, which is perfectly adequate if all your correspondents are also using PGP, but people use a variety of keyservers out on the public Internet. To that end, PGP allows you to add keyservers to its search list, so that you can find new keys more automatically in the future.

NOTE *Some keyservers are better than others, so don't add keyservers willy-nilly. PGP includes some built-in recommendations that are generally safe, and subkeys.pgp.net is reasonably reliable.*

To add a keyserver:

1. Select **Tools ▶ Edit Keyservers** to bring up the PGP Keyservers List, as shown in Figure 6-1.

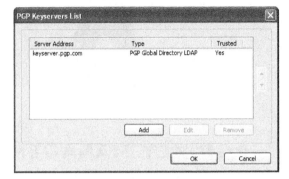

Figure 6-1: The PGP Keyservers List

2. At first, you'll see one keyserver listed. To add another, select **Add**. You'll see a screen much like Figure 6-2.

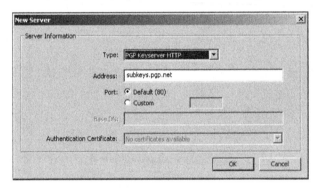

Figure 6-2: The New Server dialog box

3. PGP supports several different types of keyservers, from the LDAP used by its own Global Directory keyserver to secure LDAP used in enterprise environments, to plain old-fashioned HTTP (or Web). To use an old-fashioned OpenPGP keyserver, select a Type of **PGP Keyserver HTTP** and enter the URL in the Address space.

4. Click **OK**, and the new keyserver should appear in your list.

The entry for your new keyserver isn't exactly like the entry for keyserver.pgp.com—specifically, the space that says *Trusted* reads *No* instead of *Yes*. This is because PGP includes a copy of the public key used by the Global Directory, and all keys distributed by the PGP Global Directory have been signed by this key, providing a certain level of validation; the PGP software trusts those keys. However, average public keyservers perform no validation upon submitted keys, so those keys are not inherently trustworthy. (You can choose to find individual keys trustworthy, but their presence on a keyserver does not imply this.)

Although many people have uploaded their keys to the PGP Global Directory, you won't necessarily find every one of your correspondents there. If you find that you frequently receive messages signed or encrypted by people who do not use the PGP Global Directory, adding additional keyservers to your search will make finding public keys simpler.

At a minimum, I suggest adding subkeys.pgp.net to your keyservers list so that when PGP Desktop searches for someone's public key it will have a better chance of finding it. You might have to add other keyservers to the list as you learn more about which correspondents use which keyservers. For example, if you're at a university with its own keyserver, you will probably wind up adding that keyserver to your keyserver list.

Adding Keys to Your Keyring

After you have found someone whose identification seems correct, it's time to find, verify, and sign their key. We'll walk through this process using PGP and add this person's key to our keyring by using the email address to find the key and the fingerprint to verify that we have the correct key.

Searching Keyservers

On the left side of the PGP Desktop, under the PGP Keys heading, you should see an option to **Search for Keys**. Click it to bring up the Search for Keys screen, as shown in Figure 6-3, which allows you to build very selective queries that allow you to identify a particular key very quickly. You can search any keyserver in your system for keys that match a particular name, email address, key type, or just about any other characteristic.

The Search box allows you to choose which keyservers or local keyrings to search. (Most people only have one local keyring called *All Keys*, but if you've been playing with your software you might have more.) You can build complex searches by requiring a search to meet all, any, or none of the conditions you define below. The plus and minus signs to the right allow you to add additional conditions, including name, email address, key creation date, and so on.

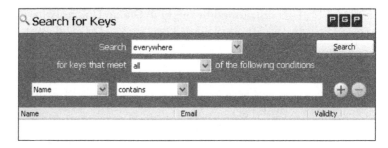

Figure 6-3: The PGP Search for Keys screen

For example, suppose that you, a PGP user, want to sign my key. You have checked my identification and the name on my key and are convinced that I am who I claim to be. I also gave you my legal name (Michael Warren Lucas, Jr.), key fingerprint (67FF 2497 8C3C C0A4 B012 DB67 C073 AC55 E68C 49BC), and email address (mwlucas@blackhelicopters .org). You'll open up your PGP Desktop, open the search screen, select the Email search option, and enter my email address in the text box.

The search screen brings up a list of all keys that contain that email address. Not surprisingly, there's only one key attached to my email address.

To add a found key to your local keyring, right-click the key and choose **Add To**, which brings up a list of keyrings your PGP software knows about. Most people have only one keyring, called *All Keys*. Choose that one, and the key will be added to your local keyring and be visible in PGP Desktop.

Importing from a File

Suppose that the key you want to sign isn't on a keyserver, but is instead distributed via some other method such as a web page. In such cases, the key is usually distributed as a file you can download.

To import a text-based key:

1. Download the key to your desktop, making sure to save it with a .asc extension so that PGP will recognize it as a key.

2. Right-click the saved file and select **Open With**. One option is to import the file with PGP Tray, a program that offers to import the key into your public keyring, so that it will be available in PGP Desktop. Choose that option.

Fingerprint Comparisons

The next step is to confirm that the key you found is the same one that I showed you. To do so:

1. Right-click the imported key and select **Properties** to open the Key Properties screen, as shown in Figure 6-4. At the bottom of the Key Properties screen, you'll see the fingerprint. (PGP provides fingerprints both in the standard hexadecimal format and a biometric format made up of words. Although the biometric format looks less intimidating, I have seen it only in software from PGP Corporation. Everybody else I know of uses hexadecimal.)

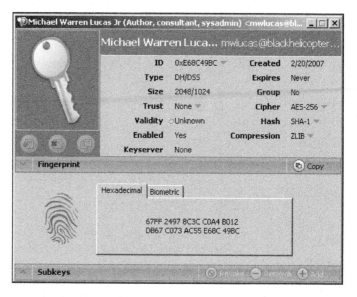

Figure 6-4: The Key Properties screen

2. Compare the entire fingerprint with that listed on the screen. (Although it might be tempting to just make sure the first four characters match, if someone was seriously attempting to impersonate me, he might well keep generating random OpenPGP keys until he got one in which a section of the fingerprint overlapped the real fingerprint, hoping that people would be too lazy to check the entire fingerprint.)

3. If the fingerprint matches, leave Key Properties and right-click the key on the search screen again.

4. Choose the first option, **Add To**, to add the key to the All Keys list.

5. Return to the main PGP Desktop screen by selecting **All Keys**, and you should see my private key added to the list.

6. Right-click the key and select **Sign** from the drop-down menu.

7. PGP displays a dialog box similar to Figure 6-5 with a strongly worded warning at the top to remind you that if you sign the key, you are providing your personal certification that the key you're signing actually belongs to the person who claims to own it.

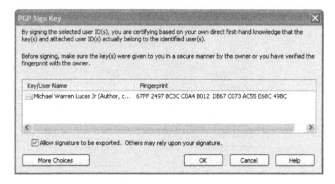

Figure 6-5: The PGP Sign Key dialog box

8. A checkbox at the bottom right of the screen says Allow Signature To Be Exported. If you're certain that you verified the key, check this box. The next time you update your keyring, your signature will be added to those on the keyserver. You'll be attaching this key owner a little more deeply into the Web of Trust. Although not strictly necessary, signing other people's keys is considered the price for getting your key signed.

9. A dialog box will request your passphrase; when you type it, you've signed the key.

10. Now return to the Key Properties screen for your newly imported key. You should see that the Validity tab now has a green dot and the word Valid beside it. While you're here, you need to decide what level of trust you have in this particular key signer (as discussed in Chapter 5). You can set the trust by simply clicking the value and choosing either **None**, **Marginal**, or **Trusted**.

Returning the Signed Key

Now that you have signed the key, return it (with your added signature) to where you got it from. If the key was distributed from a keyserver, just right-click the key in PGP Desktop and select **Synchronize** to transmit it back to the keyserver. If you got the key from a file, website, or some other method, however, you really should return it to the key owner directly. The key owner has a good reason for not publicizing a key via a keyserver. Never submit someone else's key to a keyserver!

To return the key to its owner, right-click the key entry and choose **Export**, then choose a file in which to save the exported key. Return the export file to the owner in whatever method seems best; email is OK for exported keys.

Viewing Signatures

When you add a public key to your keyring, one question to ask is "Who else has signed this key?"

To view other key signers, use the PGP Desktop. Just click the little plus sign (+) by the key to expand the key description, and you'll see a list of all the signers of that key, as shown in Figure 6-6.

Figure 6-6: Signatures on a key

Here we can see that the key for Michael Warren Lucas, Jr. has been signed by himself, by Greg Donner, and by the PGP Global Directory.

Updating Signatures

Over time, keys are revoked, are replaced, and accumulate new signatures. These changes are made available on the keyservers. Use the Synchronize Keys functions in PGP to update your keyring.

The Keys tab of the PGP Options panel (accessible under the Tools menu) includes a checkbox for automatic synchronization. If this checkbox is selected, PGP will regularly update its local keys with the latest ones from the PGP Global Directory (or any other keyserver you might have added to your system).

Adding Photos to Your Keys

Now that you're a little more conversant with the features of PGP and can wander at will through the many options PGP Desktop offers, let's add a photograph to your key. Get a digital photograph of yourself, and make sure it's in a format suitable for an OpenPGP key, as discussed in Chapter 2. Once you have a photograph ready, follow these steps:

1. Open up the Key Properties screen for your public key, as shown in Figure 6-4.

2. Right-click on the large key logo on the left-hand side and select **Add Photo**. This brings up the Add Photo dialog box, as shown in Figure 6-7.

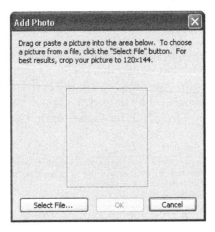

Figure 6-7: The Add Photo dialog box

3. Drag and drop your photo into this dialog box. PGP Desktop will ask for your passphrase. Once you enter your passphrase, your key will be updated with your photograph!

   To view another key's photograph, check the Key Properties for that key.

   Now that you've got a good grip on your key and the Web of Trust, let's go on to look at email and OpenPGP.

7

MANAGING GNUPG KEYS

Managing keys in GnuPG can be a little more difficult than with PGP, simply because the variety of tools don't always integrate seamlessly. We'll focus on the command-line management of keys, with some pointers to the WinPT graphic interface.

Keyservers

GnuPG allows you to choose a default keyserver, which you can override on the command line. Like so many other GnuPG features, you set your default keyserver in the gpg.conf file:

```
keyserver hkp://subkeys.pgp.net
```

The hkp stands for *Horowitz Keyserver Protocol*, which is used to exchange keys over a network. Many OpenPGP clients use HKP, but you don't need to know anything about its internals. HKP runs over TCP port 11371, so if you're behind a firewall and cannot access that port, you'll have difficulty communicating with the keyserver.

List the hostname of the keyserver after the hkp://, much like the URL for a website.

After you have added this entry into gpg.conf, GPG will assume that this is your keyserver. You can override this choice at any time with the command-line option:

```
--keyserver
```

NOTE *From here on, the examples assume that you have set a keyserver option in your gpg.conf file or your WinPT installation. If you don't want to do that but are following the examples, add the command-line option --keyserver subkeys.pgp.net to every command involving a keyserver throughout the rest of this book.*

Keyserver Options

You can tweak GnuPG's interactions with keyservers extensively. Most of those tweaks are useful only for debugging GnuPG problems, but a couple will come in handy for daily use. (Read the gpg(1) man page for the complete list of options.)

One option I find useful is automatic key retrieval. When you receive a signed or encrypted message, GnuPG checks its local keyring for a key that matches the sender of that message. If it can't find a matching key for a message that it's trying to decrypt or authenticate, GnuPG normally stops dead and waits for you to load the proper public key into your keyring. If you're lazy and don't want to search for a key by hand, you can set the keyserver option auto-key-retrieve. Although this procedure won't help if you're signing someone's key, it will make it simpler to handle exchanging documents (such as email).

Another helpful option can make GnuPG produce more detailed output about the actions it takes and any problems it encounters. If you're trying to understand how GnuPG works, either out of curiosity or in an attempt to debug a problem, you can use the verbose option to make GnuPG more chatty as it goes about its work.

```
keyserver-options auto-key-retrieve, verbose
```

Keyservers and WinPT

To see the list of keyservers in WinPT, open up Key Manager and select the **Keyserver** option from the top of the window. (Figure 4-11 shows the Key Manager with the Keyserver option.) The Keyserver Access screen will display with a list of supported keyservers, as shown in Figure 7-1.

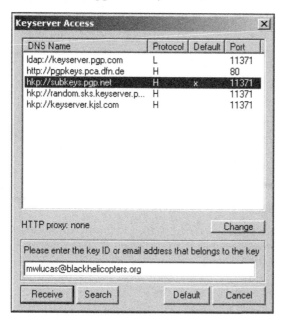

Figure 7-1: The Keyserver Access screen

You can select a default keyserver from the list by highlighting a server name and clicking **Default**. The default keyserver will then be marked with an X in the Default column. In Figure 7-1, the default keyserver is subkeys.pgp.net.

WinPT does not control its keyservers with gpg.conf. Instead, WinPT keeps its own list in C:\Program Files\GnuPT\ WPT\keyserver.conf. This is just a plain text file listing keyservers that show up in the WinPT GUI, with one keyserver per line. You must restart WinPT for changes in the keyserver list to take effect.

Adding Keys to Your Keyring

Suppose that one day you receive a digitally signed message from my email address (mwlucas@blackhelicopters.org). Although you don't need my public key to read this message, you need to get a copy of it to verify that I actually sent this message. If you're using GnuPG's automatic key retrieval, you're all set; if not, you'll need my public key's keyid to fetch the key.

If your email client doesn't display my keyid, you need to search your keyserver's web interface for it. Most keyservers, including all those that serve subkeys.pgp.net, have a web interface. If you search for keys using my email address as a search term, you'll get an answer much like this:

```
pub 1024D/E68C49BC❶ 2007-02-21❷ Michael Warren Lucas Jr (Author, consultant,
sysadmin) <mwlucas@blackhelicopters.org>❸
    Fingerprint=67FF 2497 8C3C C0A4 B012  DB67 C073 AC55 E68C 49BC ❹
```

The keyserver spits back ❶ my keyid, ❷ the date the key was created, ❸ the owner's user ID (UID), and ❹ the key fingerprint. To import the key, we need the keyid, which is E68049BC in this case.

Command-Line Key Fetching

To fetch a key using gpg from the command line, use the --recv-keys option and the keyid to download the key from your preferred keyserver, like so:

```
# gpg --recv-keys E68C49BC❶
gpg: requesting key❷ E68C49BC from hkp server subkeys.pgp.net❸
gpg: key E68C49BC: public key "Michael Warren Lucas Jr (Author,
consultant, sysadmin) <mwlucas@blackhelicopters.org>" imported❹
gpg: Total number processed: 1
gpg:               imported: 1❺
#
```

Here, we ❷ asked our preferred ❸ keyserver for the public key with the keyid ❶ E68C49BC. It responded with a public key, and it prints out ❹ the UID so that we know we got the right key. Finally, GnuPG lists ❺ the number of keys it has imported.

Command-Line Key Viewing

To view all the keys currently on your public keyring, use the gpg --list-keys option, like so:

```
# gpg --list-keys
/home/mwlucas/.gnupg/pubring.gpg❶
-------------------------------
pub❷    1024D/E68C49BC❸ 2007-02-21❹
```

```
uid                    Michael Warren Lucas Jr (Author, consul-
tant, sysadmin) <mwlucas@blackhelicopters.org>❺
sub    2048g/A67199A7 2007-02-21❻
```

GnuPG begins by printing out ❶ the name of the file in which the public key ring is kept, which should always be the pubring.gpg file in your GnuPG home directory. (Remember, we discussed the GnuPG home directory in Chapter 4.)

Next, you'll see a label for the type of key displayed; in this case, it's ❷ a public key. We have ❸ the key length and the keyid of this key, and ❹ the creation date. The key's ❺ UID is given on its own line, with any ❻ subkeys of the main OpenPGP key listed afterward. (Subkeys are keypairs that are subordinate to the main OpenPGP key, and many people highly skilled with OpenPGP have them on their keys. You generally don't have to worry about these subkeys, but don't be concerned when they appear.)

To view the keys on your private keyring, use the --list-secret-keys option.

```
# gpg --list-secret-keys
/home/mwlucas/.gnupg/secring.gpg
------------------------------
sec❶   1024D/E68C49BC 2007-02-21
uid                    Michael Warren Lucas Jr (Author, consul-
tant, sysadmin) <mwlucas@blackhelicopters.org>
ssb❷   2048g/A67199A7 2007-02-21
```

The result looks much like the public keys list, with a couple of exceptions: The private key is labeled ❶ sec for *secret*, and the subkey is labeled ❷ ssb for *secret subkey*.

As your keyrings grow, the commands --list-keys and --list-secret-keys will create multiple screens of output. In these examples, our keyring only has a single key on it: mine. If each key entry takes up only three lines, when you have nine keys on your keyring it will more than fill an average command-line window. You also don't want to have to sort through dozens or hundreds of entries to find the single key you want. To view only the entry for a single key, enter a unique key identifier after the --list option. For example, to view only my public key information, you could run the following:

```
# gpg --list-keys mwlucas@blackhelicopters.org
```

When you have hundreds of keys on your keyring, using this command to list only specific keys can make key viewing much more reasonable.

WinPT Key Viewing and Fetching

To view or fetch your keys using WinPT:

1. Open the WinPT Key Manager by double-clicking the WinPT icon in the lower-right corner of the screen. The Key Manager lists all keys (both public and private) on your keyrings. (Refer to Figure 4-11 for a diagram of the Key Manager.)

2. Click the **Keyserver** tab of the Key Manager. The Keyserver Access screen displays (refer to Figure 7-1).

3. Highlight the keyserver you want to use, enter the keyid or email address in the space at the bottom of the page, and click **Receive**. WinPT should contact your chosen keyserver, download the chosen key, and add it to your public keyring.

Command-Line Key Imports

If a public key is distributed via a method other than a keyserver (such as a website), you can bring it into GnuPG by using the --import option and the filename. For example, here's how I would import my friend Greg's public key:

```
#gpg --import❶ gedonner.asc❷
gpg: key E2F41133❸: public key "Greg Donner <gedonner@blackhelicopters.org>"❹
imported
gpg: Total number processed: 1
gpg:              imported: 1  (RSA: 1)
```

GnuPG ❶ imports the new public key from ❷ the file gedonner.asc, then prints ❸ the keyid it has found in the public key file as well as ❹ the UID.

WinPT File Imports

To import a key with WinPT:

1. Save the key file with a .asc extension.

2. Right-click the key file and select **Open With**; you should see Windows Privacy Tray (WinPT) as an option.

3. Select **Windows Privacy Tray (WinPT)**. WinPT should import the key(s) in the file and report on its results.

Signing a Key

Now that you know how to grab other people's keys from a keyserver, let's hook those keys into our Web of Trust. First, of course, you need to check the other person's ID, confirm the identity, and also note the email address and key fingerprint. After you have confirmed this information, you need to sign the public key, which involves checking the fingerprint of the downloaded public key, digitally signing the key, and then returning the key to the owner.

Checking Fingerprints

Let's assume that you imported a key that looks like the other person's key. In this example, I'm considering signing my friend Greg's key. Although I've known Greg for years, I still checked his ID and made him give me his key fingerprint. He says his fingerprint is B147 5969 B88D 3582 C05E BB83 91B5 AA6A E2F4 1133. To show the fingerprint for only his key, I use the --fingerprint option and give his email address as follows.

```
#gpg --fingerprint gedonner@blackhelicopters.org
pub   2048R/E2F41133 2007-06-25
      Key fingerprint = B147 5969 B88D 3582 C05E  BB83 91B5 AA6A E2F4 1133❶
uid                   Greg Donner <gedonner@blackhelicopters.org>
sub   2048R/8373FD79 2007-06-25
```

The output closely resembles the --list-keys output, with the addition of the line that ❶ prints the fingerprint. With this information confirmed, right-click the key in WinPT's Key Manager and select **Key Properties** to show the fingerprint. After you confirm the fingerprint, you can sign the key.

Signing Keys on the Command Line

To sign keys at the command line, use the --sign option and the keyid.

```
# gpg --sign-key E2F41133
pub   2048R/E2F41133❶  created: 2007-06-25  expires: never      usage: CS
                       trust: unknown       validity: unknown
sub   2048R/8373FD79   created: 2007-06-25  expires: never      usage: E
[ unknown] (1). Greg Donner <gedonner@blackhelicopters.org>
pub   2048R/E2F41133   created: 2007-06-25  expires: never      usage: CS
                       trust: unknown       validity: unknown
 Primary key fingerprint: B147 5969 B88D 3582 C05E  BB83 91B5 AA6A E2F4 1133❷
```

```
Greg Donner <gedonner@blackhelicopters.org>❸

Are you sure that you want to sign this key with your
key "Michael Warren Lucas Jr (Author, consultant, sysadmin) <mwlucas@
blackhelicopters.org>" (E68C49BC)

Really sign? (y/N) y❹
```

As you can see, GPG shows details about the key with the
given keyid, including ❶ the keyid, ❷ the fingerprint, and
❸ the UID of the public key. It then asks whether you really
want to sign the key with your private key. If the keyid, fingerprint, and UID match the owner's identification, ❹ enter **y**
to sign the key. You'll be prompted for your passphrase, after
which GnuPG will sign the key.

Signing Keys in WinPT

To sign keys with WinPT:

1. Right-click the key you want to sign, which should bring up
    a Key Signing dialog box that lists the fingerprint and the
    selected key's UID.

NOTE   *By default, WinPT signs keys in a* nonexportable *manner, meaning that the signature is good only for your personal Web of Trust,
but other people cannot rely on your validation. Although this might
be good safeguard for uneducated OpenPGP users, you now have a
pretty good idea of how to verify an identity. I recommend uncheck-
ing the Sign Local Only box if you are participating in the Web
of Trust and you have properly validated the key owner's identity.
(If you haven't, you shouldn't be signing the key!)*

2. Choose to enter an expiration date for the signature if you
    want, although that's not generally necessary.

3. If you have multiple private keys, WinPT allows you to
    choose which one to use for signing purposes.

4. Finally, you're asked for the passphrase for your key. Enter
    it and you should see a dialog box asking you how care-
    fully you have verified the identity of the key owner. These
    range from I Have Not Checked At All to I Have Checked
    Very Carefully. Presumably, you checked very carefully;
    check the appropriate box.

Viewing Key Signatures

After you sign a key, you should confirm that the signature is really there.

Command Line

To do this from the command line, view the signatures with the --list-sigs option and the keyid of the public key in question.

```
# gpg --list-sigs e2f41133❶
pub   2048R/E2F41133 2007-06-25
uid                   Greg Donner <gedonner@blackhelicopters.org>
sig      N  E2F41133 2007-06-25  Greg Donner <gedonner@blackhelicopters.org>❷
sig         E68C49BC 2007-07-19  Michael Warren Lucas Jr (Author, consultant,
sysadmin) <mwlucas@blackhelicopters.org>❸
sub   2048R/8373FD79 2007-06-25
sig         E2F41133 2007-06-25  Greg Donner <gedonner@blackhelicopters.org>
```

Here, we're asking for the complete list of signatures on the key with the keyid ❶ E2F41133. This key has only two signatures: one is ❷ the original owner's signature, and the other is ❸ mine.

Now, when I receive OpenPGP-encrypted or -signed mail from Greg, I know it is authentic. Presumably, Greg has also verified and signed my key, and we have our own personal Web of Trust. However, to tie each other into the public Web of Trust we must publicize the signatures on our keys. (Just remember to put the signed key back where you got it!)

WinPT

To view signatures in WinPT, right-click the key you want to check and select **View Signatures** from the drop-down menu.

To export someone else's public key that you signed, do the same as if you were exporting your own public key to a file.

Command-Line Exports

To export a public key from the command line, you'll need the keyid and a file to put it in.

```
# gpg --output❶ gedonner.asc❷ --armor❸ --export❹ E2F41133❺
```

Here, we tell GnuPG to ❶ put the results of its work in the file ❷ gedonner.asc, protect the contents with ❸ ASCII armor, and ❹ export (or copy) the public key with ❺ the keyid E2F41133 from your public keyring. This is almost identical to exporting your own public key.

This exported file includes Greg's public key, my signature of his key, and any other signatures that were on the key before I signed it. Another user can import this exported key file, either by adding the key to his keyring or by merging any new signatures onto the existing copy of that key as appropriate.

You should return the signed public key to the key owner in an encrypted, signed email and allow him to integrate your signature into his public key and then distribute it as he sees fit.

WinPT Exports

To export a key from WinPT, right-click the key in Key Manager and select **Copy Key To Clipboard**. You can then create a new text file and copy the key into it. Give the file a name indicative of its contents and a .asc extension, so other people's systems will recognize it as a proper OpenPGP public key.

Importing New Signatures

When someone sends you a file with a signature added to your public key, you add that signature onto your public key by importing the public key into your own public keyring. GnuPG will sort out the new signatures and integrate them with your public key.

Pushing Signatures to Keyservers

If you retrieved a person's public key from a keyserver, you can update the key directly on the keyserver (although only if the key has already been publicized on a keyserver!).

Command Line

To do so from the command line, use the --send-keys option to update the keyserver's record of a particular key, just as if you were first publicizing your key. Here, I refresh Greg's key (keyid E2F41133) on the keyserver:

```
# gpg --send-keys E2F41133
```

WinPT

To update a keyserver in WinPT, right-click the key in Key Manager and select **Send To Keyserver**. Then choose your default keyserver.

Updating Keys

Whenever you add signatures to your personal public key, you should announce those additional signatures using the same keyserver you uploaded your key to in the first place. Every month or so, check your keyring to confirm that the keys you downloaded previously are still valid and to update your copies with any additional signatures that your keys have collected. You can do so with the --refresh-keys option.

```
# gpg --refresh-keys
gpg: refreshing ❶31 keys from ❷hkp://subkeys.pgp.net
gpg: requesting key ❸D4ED7B9F from hkp server subkeys.pgp.net
gpg: requesting key ...
...
```

GnuPG announces ❶ the number of keys on your public keyring and ❷ the keyserver it is trying to check them against, and then lists each key by ❸ keyid as it tries to fetch each from the keyserver. If a key is not on the keyserver, you'll see a brief notice like this:

```
1718CCCE595F038CA0D83C12EC398AB271 not found on keyserver
```

In this example, I installed this particular key from an exported file, and the key is not available on a keyserver. To check this key for new signatures, I need to return to where I got the key from in the first place and get a new public key file.

NOTE *If a key has changed, GnuPG will display those changes and update the copy of that key on your public keyring.*

At the end of the update process, GnuPG prints the number of keys it's checked, the number of unchanged keys, and the number of new signatures it has found.

Deleting Public Keys from Your Keyring

If you have refused to sign a public key for whatever reason, you probably don't want it on your public keyring. The same goes for the public key of someone with whom you no longer correspond.

Command Line

To delete a public key from your keyring, use the --delete-key option and the keyid.

```
# gpg --delete-keys E2F41133

pub  2048R/E2F41133 2007-06-25 Greg Donner <gedonner@blackhelicopters.org>

Delete this key from the keyring? (y/N) y
```

GnuPG gives you every chance to double-check the key that you want to delete by presenting the keyid and its UID before requesting confirmation. If this really is the key you want to delete, enter **y**, and the key will disappear from your public keyring.

WinPT

To delete a key from WinPT, right-click the key in Key Manager and select **Delete**.

GnuPG and Photos

GnuPG can add photos to OpenPGP keys and view the keys on other people's keys. Photo IDs can be a nice addition to your OpenPGP key, as discussed in Chapter 2. Now that you know a little more about GnuPG and key management, you can add photos to your own key and view photos on other users' keys.

Adding Photos to Your Key

GnuPG includes a very sophisticated and powerful keypair editor. This editor gives you the power to tweak your key in any way you can imagine. Most of these tweaks will render an average user's key useless, so I won't cover the editor in any depth. You must use this editor to add a photo, however. Enter the editor with the --edit-key option and your keyid or email address.

```
# gpg --edit-key mwlucas@blackhelicopters.org

Secret key is available.❶

pub  1024D/E68C49BC❷  created: 2007-02-21  expires: never       usage: CS
                      trust: ultimate       validity: ultimate
sub  2048g/A67199A7  created: 2007-02-21  expires: never       usage: E
[ultimate] (1). Michael Warren Lucas Jr (Author, consultant, sysadmin) <mwlucas@
blackhelicopters.org>❸
Command>❹
```

GnuPG will tell you that you have ❶ the secret key for the key you're choosing to edit—which you certainly should, as it's your key! It will also list ❷ the keyid and ❸ the UID of this key. Make sure that this is your key before continuing. Finally, GnuPG will provide ❹ a command prompt for the editor. Use the addphoto command.

```
Command>addphoto
```

```
Pick an image to use for your photo ID. The image must be a
JPEG file. Remember that the image is stored within your public
key. If you use a very large picture, your key will become very
large as well! Keeping the image close to 240x288 is a good size
to use.
```

```
Enter JPEG filename for photo ID: c:/temp/photo.jpg
```

When GnuPG asks for the filename for the photo, give the full name including the path. (You don't need the full path if you're running the command from the directory where the file can be found, but I usually specify the full path just to be certain.) GnuPG will launch an image viewer to show the picture. Look at the picture and make sure that it's really the photo of you that you wish to advertise to the world. If this picture is correct, exit the image viewer. GnuPG will prompt you again:

```
Is this photo correct (y/N/q)? y
```

GnuPG will then request your passphrase, to prove that you are actually allowed to make this change. Enter your passphrase.

```
Command> save
```

This will return you to a command prompt. If you made a mistake, you can enter quit instead of save to abort the change.

Viewing Photos with GnuPG

You must use a graphical operating system to view photos with GnuPG. This includes Microsoft Windows or Unix-like operating systems running X Windows. To view a photograph attached to a key, use the --list-options show-photo command-line option before --list-keys.

```
# gpg --list-options show-photos --list-keys
mwlucas@blackhelicopters.org
```

This will display the information for my key and launch an image viewer to display the picture in your chosen key. Be careful that you don't just list all the keys on your keyring; chances are that many of those keys have a picture, and you'll spawn a separate image viewer for each key with a picture. If you have a large keyring, this opens dozens if not hundreds of images!

WinPT and Photos

To add a photo to your keypair using WinPT, open the WinPT Key Manager (as shown in Figure 4-11 on page 65). Right-click on your key, and choose **Add . . .**

From the Add submenu, select **Photo**. WinPT will open the Add Photo ID dialog box as shown in Figure 7-2.

Figure 7-2: The Add Photo ID dialog box

Give the full path to your photo and enter your passphrase. WinPT will add the photo to your key.

To view a photo with WinPT, double-click on the photo in Key Manager. The Key Properties dialog box will appear, as shown in Figure 7-3.

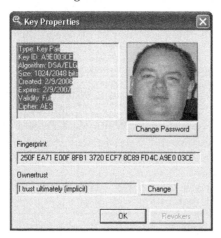

Figure 7-3: The Key Properties dialog box with a photograph

WinPT is perhaps the easiest way to handle photos with GnuPG.

Building the Web of Trust with GnuPG

Now that you know how to manage your keyring, let's build our Web of Trust with GnuPG.

PGP

You saw in Chapter 6 that PGP's trust model is very straightforward: If a public key is signed by someone whose key you have signed, that key is trusted, which makes it very easy to build a Web of Trust with PGP.

GnuPG

GnuPG is a little more paranoid (or, if you prefer, "proper"). You can assign degrees of trust to every public key on your keyring (as I discussed at the tail end of Chapter 5). For GnuPG to trust a previously unknown key, that key must be signed by one fully trusted person or three marginally trusted people. Remember, this is *not* trust as in "Here, hold my winning lottery ticket." We're specifically talking about the person's ability to validate the identity of others and their consistency in doing so correctly. You can assign your trust of a particular key with either the command line or WinPT.

GnuPG stores trust information in the file $GPGHOME/trustdb.gpg. Trust information is independent from the public keys themselves because we all trust different people to different degrees.

NOTE   *Update the trust database regularly to keep this from becoming an overwhelming job. It's much easier to add trust values for the half-dozen new OpenPGP users you talked to in the last week than to add them for the hundreds of people you corresponded with in the last year!*

Command-Line Trust Configuration

Use the --update-trustdb option to assign a trust level to every key on your public keyring. This command will iterate over every key in your public keyring and give you an opportunity to assign a trust value to each one.

```
# gpg --update-trustdb
...
Please decide how far you trust this user to correctly verify other users' keys
(by looking at passports, checking fingerprints from different sources, etc.)
```

```
1 = I don't know or won't say
2 = I do NOT trust
3 = I trust marginally
4 = I trust fully
s = skip this key
q = quit
```

Your decision? **1**

GnuPG will display the basic information for each key, including its UID and fingerprint, and then ask you to choose how much you trust this person's ability to identify other OpenPGP users. Pick the appropriate value for each person in your keyring, and GnuPG will build your personal Web of Trust based on your preferences.

If you're in any doubt whatsoever about a key, use "I don't know or won't say," which allows you to use those keys without making any commitments to trusting the user.

WinPT Trust Configuration

To configure trust in WinPT:

1. Right-click the key in Key Manager and select **Key Properties**.

2. At the bottom of the dialog box, you'll see a space labeled *Ownertrust.* Select the **Change** button to assign a level of trust to this owner.

Now that you have trust, let's see how OpenPGP works with email.

8

OPENPGP AND EMAIL

Learning how OpenPGP works and how to use it to manage your keyring has just been a warm-up to the real meat of this book: using OpenPGP with email.

Both PGP and GnuPG extend mail programs to include OpenPGP functions. As you'll soon see, OpenPGP operations in all mail programs are very similar after you learn where your particular client puts the "encrypt" and "sign" buttons. After you can use one OpenPGP program with a particular email client, you can extend that knowledge to cover other email clients.

Back in Chapter 1, we had a table that listed all the actions you could perform with OpenPGP. That was before you knew words such as *nonrepudiation*, however, and so it might not have meant as much to you as it does now. Take a look at it again here (Table 8-1) with your newfound cryptographic wisdom, and see how public keys, private keys, and digital signatures all tie together to create a chosen level of privacy. After you begin working with OpenPGP on a daily basis, it won't take long to learn when to use the six features in Table 8-1.

Table 8-1: Key Usages

Desired Effect	Action
I want anyone who reads this message to know beyond a doubt that I sent it—I cannot repudiate it.	Digitally sign the message with your private key.
I want to verify the identity of the person who sent a digitally signed message to see whether the apparent sender is the real sender.	Verify the signature with the sender's public key.
I want to send a message that only my intended recipient can read.	Encrypt the message with the recipient's public key.
I want to decrypt a message that I received.	Decrypt the message with your private key.
I want my message to be readable only by my intended recipient, and I want the recipient to be able to verify that the message came from me.	Encrypt the message with the recipient's public key and digitally sign the message with your private key.
I want to decrypt and verify a message that includes a digital signature.	Decrypt the message with your private key and verify the signature with the sender's public key.

Message Encoding

When used with email, OpenPGP uses two different methods to encode messages. PGP/MIME is the more modern choice, being attachment-based, but not all mail clients support it. The older *inline encoding*, also known as *clearsigning*, works well for basic email messages. The choice of encoding varies with different email clients and OpenPGP programs, and I'll discuss the options in the following sections.

Inline Encoding

Inline encoding occurs directly within the body of the email message. When you sign a message with inline encoding, the message body is edited to include an OpenPGP signature at the very end of the message. When encrypting and signing a message, the encrypted message replaces the original message body completely.

If you open an inline-encrypted message without using an OpenPGP program, it will start off looking much like the following:

```
-----BEGIN PGP MESSAGE-----
Version: PGP Desktop 9.0.2 (Build 2433)

qANQR1DBwU4D2jTKQaZxmacQCACbxrL+clBol8wB1R16tr5vXFFLurHsug9Qk6Cq
...
```

Not much to look at if you can't decode it.

Inline Encryption Trade-Offs

Inline encryption is about as simple as you can get, but as time has passed, its limitations have become more and more apparent. Inline encryption can have trouble with non-English character sets, attachments, and binary documents.

Non-English character sets (such as the symbols used for Chinese or Russian text) can cause problems for inline encryption. Email was designed by English speakers for English speakers, and mail programs already jump through hoops to manage non-English character sets.[1] Combining these characters with OpenPGP can cause unpredictable effects, depending on your combination of email client and OpenPGP software.

Similarly, attachments can be problematic with inline encryption. Your email client might encrypt your message body but leave the attachment unencrypted. To use inline encryption in such a case, you would need to encrypt your attachment separately and attach the signature and the encrypted attachment to the message. Also, when using inline encryption, you cannot encode binary data, such as PDFs, Microsoft Word documents, digital photos, and so on.

Finally, as if all this weren't enough, mail servers can corrupt clearsigned messages.

On the other hand, in spite of these challenges with inline encryption, OpenPGP-signed messages that use inline encoding can be read by any mail client.

When you use inline encryption, you must be aware of how your mail client interacts with your OpenPGP software in these circumstances. We discuss these interactions in the next two

---

[1] I like to think that if the original creators of email realized that it would be used by people all over the world instead of just a handful of highly skilled engineers, they would have anticipated these problems and designed around them. Then again, if the creators had realized what their innocent tool would become, they might have just given up the whole thing as a bad idea and bought extra stamps.

chapters. In a nutshell, PGP Corporation puts a lot of work into making inline encryption work properly and easily for everyone, whereas GnuPG varies with different clients.

PGP/MIME was designed to address all these issues and handle these cases without trouble.

PGP/MIME

If you're a computer geek, you've probably seen the expression *MIME type* before. MIME, or Multipurpose Internet Mail Extension, is a whole set of standards for encoding email. PGP/MIME is the encoding method designed for OpenPGP email. PGP/MIME gets around the problems with inline encryption by treating absolutely everything as an attachment: The encrypted message is sent as an attachment, the signed message and signatures are sent as attachments, and anything you attach is encrypted and attached.

Mail servers and mail clients treat attachments and email messages differently: Mail servers never modify attachments, and mail clients treat attachments as separate objects. Because attachments are left alone, PGP/MIME makes it much simpler to encrypt messages that use different character sets or binary files.

Generally speaking, all email clients, as well as Open-PGP implementations, can read both inline and PGP/MIME encoding unless otherwise noted in the program. PGP will handle each type of encoding, whereas GnuPG has limitations depending on the mail client you're using. Some mail clients work better with GnuPG than others.

OTHER ENCODINGS

Many people and companies have created their own email security systems in the last two decades. Most of these systems have received limited acceptance, whereas others were popular for a time and then disappeared. You might see references to these other encoding systems, such as S/MIME. Some mail clients include support for S/MIME, but that's not OpenPGP.

If you're exploring your email program and find a checkbox that says something about S/MIME, you're in the wrong spot.

Email Client Integration

You can integrate OpenPGP with your email client using either proxies or plug-ins.

Proxies

A *proxy* is a small program that runs on your computer and sits between your email client and your mail server. The proxy sends and receives email sent to your mail server, and the mail client sends and receives mail only through the proxy.

Proxies work with any mail client, but they are not as tightly integrated with the client as most people want; you configure signing, encryption, and decryption in the proxy program rather than in the mail client. Too, when using a proxy, you won't get an "encrypt and sign" button or menu option in your email client; instead, you'll have to open the proxy program and say "Encrypt all messages now" or "Encrypt messages to this email address." (PGP uses a proxy to handle messages, as I'll discuss in Chapter 9.)

Plug-Ins

The other option is *plug-ins*, which are used by GnuPG. A plug-in integrates with your email client, providing "sign" and "encrypt" buttons directly within the client.

Each mail client plug-in is unique, which means that a plug-in designed for Microsoft Outlook will not work in Mozilla Thunderbird.

Because plug-ins are written separately, each behaves slightly differently and has a different interface. Usually, the plug-in is written to look like it's part of the mail client program; integration is the whole point, after all! (I'll discuss GnuPG plug-ins for the three most popular Windows email clients in Chapter 10.)

Saving Email—Encrypted or Not?

Like many people, I save all my old email[2] because I find it very useful for reference. In fact, I've worked at companies in which saving every piece of email from your manager was the only way you could keep your job longer than a month.

OpenPGP presents some interesting problems when archiving mail, however. For example, when you send someone encrypted email, the reader must use the recipient's private key to read it. However, because you don't have the recipient's

---

[2] I have a complete archive of my email since 1985, minus only pieces that I have deliberately chosen to delete. I suspect that the mere existence of this archive will be submitted as evidence at my eventual sanity hearing. That or my publisher will publish it all. I mean, the guy published a book containing nothing but messages written *to* spammers! I can't imagine who let him out of his cage, let alone gave him a job.

private key, you can't read the mail that you sent, even though you created it!

Saving Unencrypted Email

Some email client plug-ins allow you to save mail as unencrypted. The problem with choosing this option is that it will protect your email during transit and while on the recipient's computer, but not on your hard drive. Anyone who can access your computer will be able to read those encrypted messages.

Although this option might be fine in a corporate environment, if you're in a totalitarian country being threatened by some ugly man with a rusty machete and serious anger issues, those messages just might mean life and death (for your correspondents, if not for you). (I wish this were a joke; in fact, OpenPGP has saved lives in exactly this situation.)

One popular option is to save all your email unencrypted, but on an encrypted disk partition. We discuss this briefly in Chapter 11.

Encrypt to Self

Another popular option is to also "encrypt to self" (in other words, to encrypt the saved email with your public key so that you can open it using your private key and passphrase). Using this option will stop people from getting the document even if your computer is stolen, and it is often a good middle ground for many people. (You can get the same effect in an email client that saves sent mail as encrypted by Cc-ing yourself when you send the original message.)

NOTE *If you're using a proxy program to provide OpenPGP services, the mail client will see only unencrypted emails. This means that your mail is always saved unencrypted.*

We'll discuss which options each piece of software provides (if any) in the next two chapters.

Email from Beyond Your Web of Trust

People across the world use OpenPGP, and you don't know all of them. Chances are that your keyring will start off populated with keys for friends and coworkers, and slowly grow as you communicate with more OpenPGP users. If you receive an encrypted email from a country on the far side of the world, however, it's quite possible that you will have nobody in common and hence you won't really be able to truly verify their identity. What do you do?

One possibility is to use only the corporate PGP keyserver and only correspond with people who use that keyserver. PGP Corporation's keyserver signs public keys after it verifies the email address they're attached to.

However, OpenPGP is called "open" because anyone can implement it, and you can't control who will send you email any more than you can control who sends you postcards. I correspond with people all over the world who use OpenPGP, and quite a few have public keys that aren't even vaguely hooked into my Web of Trust. How can I trust them? Here are my three choices:

- Expand my Web of Trust
- Trace the Web of Trust to that person
- Use the key but limit my trust of the sender

Expanding Your Web of Trust

The most correct answer is to expand your Web of Trust. Exchange signatures with more people, even people with whom you're not likely to exchange encrypted mail. More people than you suspect travel between companies, countries, continents, and cultures. Sign their keys and have them sign yours, which will embed you more deeply in the Web of Trust, making it easier for you to reach others and for others to reach you. This takes time, however, and if you receive a mysterious email you don't want to wait weeks or months to read it.

Tracing the Web of Trust

Search Google for "PGP pathfinder" and you'll find any number of websites in which you can trace the path through the Web of Trust between any two OpenPGP keys available on public keyservers. These sites use the keyid for the two keys involved (remember, the keyid is just the last eight characters of the fingerprint). The more paths that exist through different people, the more likely I am to trust that key. Having had my key signed at a couple of different keysigning parties, I would expect to have several paths to anyone in the Web of Trust.

For example, suppose that after publishing this book I get an email from someone who claims to be Phil Zimmermann, the original creator of PGP. The keyid of the message sender is B2D7795E. I can grab Phil Zimmermann's public key from a keyserver, or from his web page, but it's possible that someone uploaded a bogus key for him just to fool people like me.

I visit the Web of Trust pathfinder at www.cs.uu.nl/people/ henkp/henkp/pgp/pathfinder (Google's first result) and enter the keyid of the message I received and my keyid. This server tells me that there are eight *disjunct* paths between this key and mine. In other words, my key is linked to the other key by eight different paths that have *no people whatsoever in common*. For that key to be fake, the faker would have had to fool a whole lot of people. Although I have never met Phil Zimmermann, I would believe that this key is legitimate. (If the only path had been through one of my incorrigible practical joker friends, or if there had only been one path, I would have been far more suspicious and infinitely less trusting.)

Most of these Web of Trust tracing programs are based on *wotsap*, a freely available Python program designed to trace relationships between keys. Wotsap is available at many Internet sites; if you're seriously interested in analyzing the Web of Trust, I suggest you start there.

Repeatable Anonymity

No matter what you do, one day you will receive an OpenPGP-encrypted message from someone you don't know, whose key you cannot verify, and who is not in the Web of Trust. What do you do?

Well, you have three choices. One, you can delete the message unread. Two, you can leave the message sitting around until you can verify the owner's identity. Three, you can install the sender's public key and read the mail, which is actually perfectly safe.

"Safe? How can it be safe, when you can't verify the identity of the sender?" Because installing any public key is harmless: An unknown key on your public keyring won't cause your machine to be insecure, can't leak your passphrase to the world, and won't allow Mallory to steal your bank records. (Yes, Mallory could find a "magic public key" that would expose a software bug in your OpenPGP implementation and use it to crack your machine wide open, but both PGP and GnuPG handle keys very cautiously and are audited for just such problems.)

Untrusted, unknown keys that aren't attached to your Web of Trust can actually be extremely useful for anonymous or pseudonymous communications. For example, when I began this book I asked for technical reviewers on various OpenPGP-related mailing lists. A person who regularly made valuable contributions to a GnuPG list under a fairly obvious pseudonym offered to read the book. I have no idea who this person is in the real world. I have no idea of his credentials, other than his intelligent contributions to the list. I don't even know if he is really a he, she, it, or perhaps even a hyperintelligent mouse who is attempting to engage me in his latest overcomplicated plan to take over the world. I have this person's OpenPGP public key, however. When I receive an email signed or encrypted with that key, I know that the sender has the matching private key and passphrase. The author is pseudonymous, and yet I know that he's the same person every time. An impostor who wanted to assume this person's identity would have to get the passphrase and private key from the real person, and then be able to write email in the same style and with the same knowledge as the original person.

This feature is very useful for anyone who has to deal with anonymous sources on a regular basis or who wants to remain anonymous for the present but reserve the option of proving their identity later. For example, imagine a corporate whistleblower who wants to anonymously leak information. A string of OpenPGP-signed messages is a perfect way to do this. The whistleblower can distribute incriminating documents, all signed with OpenPGP. After the corporate giant is destroyed and the CEO carted off to jail for being really, really naughty, the whistleblower can prove that he was the document source by producing the private key and passphrase—or not.

The real question here is "How far do you trust?" Adding a key to your keyring doesn't mean you have to sign it or believe what the email's author writes; it only means you can read the sender's message and make up your own mind. If you decide that the person is full of baloney, you can remove the key from your keyring and have your email client delete further messages unread. If you decide to correspond with the person further, at least you know that subsequent messages are from the same person.

If you can use keys disconnected from the Web of Trust, does this make the Web of Trust less useful? Not at all; the Web of Trust is wonderful for verifying the identities of correspondents, especially when you use path tracing. The Web of Trust is a great way to verify that you are who you claim to be.

By the same token, the Web of Trust is not a straitjacket; using OpenPGP without the Web of Trust provides different possibilities. Without the Web of Trust, trying to prove someone's identity is like searching at midnight in a coal cellar for a black cat that isn't there. The Web of Trust gives you a net and a flashlight, or at least tells you that the cat might be a tiger.

Unprotected Email Components

OpenPGP goes through any number of hoops to protect the contents of the message, but you should remember what it doesn't protect. In particular, OpenPGP does not encrypt the subject lines in email. A subject such as "Ransom pickup at 8PM, City Park" doesn't leave many questions for anyone who intercepts your email. Email messages sent with PGP should have innocuous subjects (or perhaps no subject at all).

Also, your mail client might default to storing unencrypted versions of the OpenPGP emails that you send. Be sure that you know how your OpenPGP system stores messages. My preferred OpenPGP mail client (mutt) stores the sent messages in encrypted format, which means that I cannot read messages that I have sent unless I Cc myself. Some people find this irritating, and configure their mail clients to store sent messages in unencrypted format.

This really is a matter of what best suits your needs. If you are unconcerned about someone who gets access to your computer being able to read your sent mails, fine. If you are in a life-threatening situation, however, it is best to keep your sent messages encrypted, as I'll discuss in the next two chapters.

You now know enough to actually use OpenPGP and the Web of Trust in day-to-day work. Let's see how to configure email clients under both GnuPG and PGP.

9

PGP AND EMAIL

PGP makes email use as easy as possible by managing much of OpenPGP's complexity for you, so it is an excellent choice as an email plug-in for people who want encrypted email to "just work." The PGP Corporation is committed to making OpenPGP simple to use.

One way that PGP makes managing email easy is through policy-based encryption and signing rules. You define rules that dictate how PGP treats messages, and the software will automatically encrypt and sign emails as you require. PGP transparently intercepts all the email you send and receive, processes it according to your policies, and reinjects the messages into the email system for processing. This process works with any email client and eliminates any chance of your saying "Oops! I forgot to encrypt that last message!"

PGP and Your Email Client

Configuring your email client to work with PGP is simple. After you install PGP Desktop, the program lurks in the background, waiting for you to send an email. When it detects an email in progress, PGP Desktop will intercept the request and display a dialog box asking if you want to secure this email account. Answer **Yes** and go to the next screen. You'll be asked to choose between generating a new PGP key, using your existing PGP Desktop key, or importing a PGP keypair. Choose **PGP Desktop Key** and select your private key from the list. That's it! You have configured this email account to work with PGP.

> Be sure to run PGP Desktop any time you send email. If your PGP proxy is shut off, it cannot intercept your mail for you. Any mail you send will be unencrypted and you cannot read any encrypted mail you receive! What's more, you might not even notice that your outgoing mail isn't encrypted. Watch for the little padlock icon of PGP Desktop in the lower-right corner of your desktop.

If you have problems with PGP intercepting your email, your mail client is probably using a secure connection to your mail server. These secure connections, also called *SSL connections*, prevent PGP from proxying your email. Check your email account settings; most email clients have a dialog window in which you enter your email servers and a checkbox labeled something similar to This Server Requires A Secure Connection. Confirm that box is not checked. If your mail server offers Secure Sockets Layer (SSL) connections, PGP Desktop will automatically detect that capability and use it, but you cannot let your mail client handle that itself.

Identifying OpenPGP Mail

Because all OpenPGP activity is handled entirely by the proxy, your email client is not involved in the PGP process. Received messages appear entirely in cleartext, but the PGP proxy adds a line like this to the top of the message:

```
* PGP Signed: 9/22/07 at 11:45:28
```

At the end of the message, PGP adds two additional lines, listing the user ID (UID) of the author and the keyid.

For example, a message from me would include the following:

```
* Michael Warren Lucas Jr (Author, consultant, sysadmin)
* 0xE68C49BC
```

These lines are the only notice within the email message that PGP was involved, so be sure to watch for them!

Email Storage

Another side effect of an email proxy is that all email is stored unencrypted on your local computer. If you have confidential data in your email and computer theft is a concern, be sure to protect the email on your hard drive. PGP Desktop has features to encrypt and decrypt files and folders that you might wish to use to encrypt your entire mail archive. You'd have to unencrypt the mail archive to send and receive mail, of course, but in some circumstances that's safer than having your email public. (PGP Desktop's Virtual Disk software allows you to encrypt and decrypt partitions or create encrypted *virtual partitions*, which are encrypted files that can be used to store data much like a virtual floppy disk.)

PGP Policies

PGP Desktop doesn't add any buttons to your email client, so when using it you can't decide within the client whether to encrypt or sign particular messages. Those decisions are all made in the proxy, which is configured via PGP Desktop. This ensures that your use of PGP is consistent; you cannot forget to encrypt a confidential message after you tell PGP Desktop that messages of that type are confidential. To manage the proxy you must know how to create and manage PGP policies. To manage your PGP policies, open the **PGP Desktop** and select the **Messaging** tab. You should see two policy options: New Messaging Policy and Edit Policy. The main window of PGP Desktop also shows your current policy list, as shown in Figure 9-1.

PGP Desktop includes several default policies. These defaults will suffice for most people, but you must understand them to use PGP successfully. The four policies included in PGP 9.0 are Opportunistic Encryption, Require Encryption, Mailing List Submissions, and Mailing List Admin Requests (discussed in the following sections).

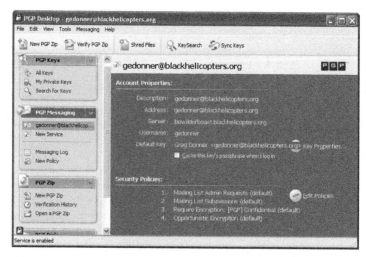

Figure 9-1: PGP Messaging showing active security policies

Opportunistic Encryption

Opportunistic Encryption simply means "Use a key for a particular recipient if you can find it." If you receive email from a particular correspondent and your keyring has a public key for this person, PGP will use that key to encrypt the message before sending. However, if your keyring has no key for this person, PGP will consult its keyservers for an appropriate key and use it if found. (By default, PGP uses the PGP Global Directory keyserver, which works perfectly for corresponding with any PGP user and with OpenPGP users who have submitted their keys to this keyserver. See Chapter 6 for instructions on adding additional keyservers, if desired.) If no public key is found for this correspondent, PGP sends the message unsigned and unencrypted.

Require Encryption

Require Encryption tells PGP that a message to a particular recipient must be encrypted. If PGP cannot encrypt the message, the message is rejected; when you click **Send**, you'll see a warning somewhat like this:

An error occurred while sending mail. The mail server responded:
No encryption key found for recipient: mwlucas@blackhelicopters
.org. Please check the message and try again.

This tells you that PGP intercepted this message but could not find a public key for the recipient, so it rejected the message.

To activate the Require Encryption policy, put the string [PGP] (including the square brackets) somewhere in the subject of your email. PGP will see this string and engage the policy.

Mailing List Submissions

The *Mailing List Submissions* policy is designed to catch emails to mailing lists because messages sent to a public forum should never be encrypted (after all, whose key would you use?). You can still sign these messages, however, so that everyone knows that they really are from you.

The Mailing List Submissions policy is controlled by the email address you are sending mail to. As of this writing, any email address containing -users@, -bugs@, -docs@, -help@, -news@, -digest@, -list@, -devel@, and -announce@ is handled by this policy. (To see the current list for your version of PGP, select **Messaging ▸ Edit Policy ▸ Mailing List Submissions**.)

For example, I subscribe to the NetBSD-users mailing list, with an email address of netbsd-users@netbsd.org. Any mail I send to this address will be signed but not encrypted.

NOTE   *This policy doesn't cover all possible email mailing lists, of course, but we'll learn how to add a custom policy later.*

Mailing List Admin Requests

Finally, the *Mailing List Admin Requests* policy is used when managing subscriptions to mailing lists (many mailing lists are managed via email messages).

How often have you seen an instruction such as "Send mail to subscribe@vendor.com to get on our mailing list"? The programs that read these emails cannot understand OpenPGP, and might interpret your signed or encrypted email unpredictably.

This PGP policy handles requests to any email address that contains -subscribe@, -unsubscribe@, -report@, -request@, and -bounces@. (To see the current list for your version of PGP, select **Messaging ▸ Edit Policy ▸ Mailing List Admin Requests**.)

These four policies are processed in order, with the first matching policy having precedence. To see the current policy order, select **PGP Messaging** from the left side of the PGP Desktop to display the list of security policies.

NOTE   *To change the order in which the policies are processed, choose **Edit Policies** on the right of the policy list.*

Creating Custom Policies

Not surprisingly, almost everyone's email activity is more complicated than four simple rules can express. You'll have correspondents to whom you will want to send only signed (not encrypted) messages, even if they have a public key on a keyserver; you might have other correspondents with an email address that matches another policy but to whom you want to send only unencrypted and unsigned mail because they're confused by encryption or signatures. For these special cases, you will need to create custom policies. To create a custom policy in PGP Desktop, select **Messaging ▸ New Messaging Policy** to display a blank Message Policy template like the one shown in Figure 9-2.

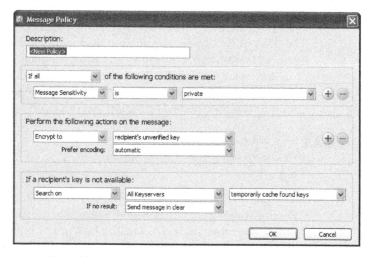

Figure 9-2: A blank Message Policy template

Enter a description of your policy in the Description field. You must then define the conditions under which the policy will take effect, the actions that will be taken when the conditions are met, and what to do if the desired actions fail.

Conditions

The first section describes the conditions under which the policy will be applied. You can define several conditions and declare that if all, any, or none of the conditions are met the policy will apply. PGP lets you build conditions based on the email's recipient, recipient domain, message subject, message header, message body, message priority, or message sensitivity, all available through drop-down boxes. For example, you could say that if the message is sent to a particular address with a particular subject, it must be encrypted, but that otherwise messages should pass in cleartext. Let's look at each of these options and see when and how they might be used.

- The *Recipient* is the email address of the person with whom you are corresponding. For example, you might create a policy to dictate that any message to me, mwlucas@blackhelicopters.org, must be encrypted and signed. (Of course, the Opportunistic Encryption default policy should make this happen for you, anyway.)

- Similarly, the *Recipient Domain* is the domain name of the email address of the person with whom you are corresponding. For example, the Recipient Domain for my email address (mwlucas@blackhelicopters.org) is blackhelicopters.org. As another example, you might want to send all email to a service such as Gmail unencrypted; Gmail does not offer PGP tools.

- The *Message Subject* option allows you to choose message subjects that will trigger encryption. For example, you could write a rule that says, "Any message with a subject of Secret Project must be encrypted and signed," much like the default policy in which any message with a subject of [PGP] must be encrypted and signed. When you compose a message with a subject of *Secret Project*, PGP will automatically intercept, sign, encrypt, and transmit that message for you.

- Some mail clients allow you to insert customized message *headers* into your email messages. You can write a policy that acts depending upon the content of those headers. If you don't know what message headers are, don't worry about it; you don't need to understand email headers to use PGP.

- *Message Priority* and *Message Sensitivity* are set within the mail client when you compose a message. Most clients will offer these options, though frequently they're difficult to locate. However, this sort of filtering is better managed by either recipient or subject rules. For example, you could write a policy that says "If the sensitivity is confidential or greater, encrypt and sign."

After you have set your conditions, you can determine whether the policy requires all conditions to be met, any of the conditions to be met, or none of the conditions to be met. The plus sign next to the condition description lets you add additional terms.

Actions

The next section in the Message Policy dialog box, Perform The Following Actions On The Message, tells PGP Desktop what to do when the conditions you set are met. Your choices are either Sign, Encrypt, or Send In Cleartext.

If this policy sends email in cleartext, you're done.

If you choose to encrypt or sign messages that fit this policy, you can also choose which sort of encoding you wish to use for this message. (We discussed inline and PGP/MIME encoding in Chapter 8.)

If you choose to encrypt matching messages, you can choose which key to use to encrypt the message. The default option is an Unverified Key, meaning a key that you have not personally signed. A Verified Key is one that you have signed. You can also explicitly encrypt the message with an explicit list of public keys.

Exceptions

If your policy encrypts matching messages, you must decide what to do if PGP Desktop does not already have a key for that recipient. You can have PGP Desktop search for the key, send the message in cleartext, or block the message.

By default, PGP Desktop will search all configured keyservers for a public key for this recipient. If it finds a matching key, it will automatically download it and encrypt the message with that key. If it does not find a matching key, you can have PGP either send the message in cleartext anyway or block the message entirely. This option is generally the most useful.

With the Send In Clear option you can make PGP Desktop not search for a matching key on a keyserver, but just send the message unencrypted anyway, even though you explicitly stated earlier that this message must be encrypted. For example, suppose that your policy says that all email with a subject of Secret Project must be encrypted. If you do not have a key for the recipient on your keyring and you select this action, the message will be sent unencrypted anyway.

You can also have PGP block the message entirely if it doesn't have a key already on its keyring. This makes sense in high-security situations in which you must retain control over the spread of information and the contents of your keyring.

Sample Custom Policy: Exceptions to Default Policy

In most cases, PGP Desktop's default policies are sufficient. The cases in which I find custom policies most useful are when

I need to make a particular exception to a policy or I want to change a default policy.

For example, I work with a software vendor who has a support mailing address of software-users@vendor.com, which happens to match an address used in the Mailing List Submissions policy, which tells PGP Desktop to sign the message. When I sign an email to this address, however, one of its support people inevitably asks me about the "stuff" at the end of the message. It might be clearly labeled BEGIN PGP SIG-NATURE, but this $8/hour support guy, whose previous job involved industrial lawn equipment (plus, if he had seniority, perhaps a bandana), has never heard of PGP. I don't have the energy to educate the staff, so it's easier to simply not sign messages to that address. To do so, I must create a custom policy to override the default policy.

Similarly, I have a friend who published an OpenPGP key several years ago but who no longer uses any sort of PGP software. I must tell PGP to never encrypt mail to him, no matter what, because he won't be able to read it.[1] I can handle both situations with a custom policy, as shown in Figure 9-3.

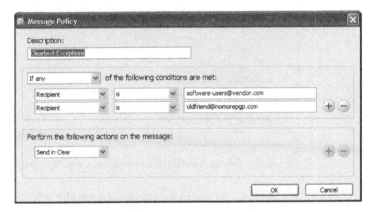

Figure 9-3: Custom PGP Message Policy

This custom policy ensures that any mail to the vendor will be sent unencrypted and unsigned, making life easier for both the support people and myself. My friend's email address is also on this list.

NOTE   *Because I selected Send In Clear, all the options about key processing have vanished.*

---

[1] If he had been sufficiently wise to put an expiration date on his key, this would not be a problem.

I could expand this policy as I discover more people who should never receive OpenPGP mail from me.

Sample Custom Policy: Overriding the Defaults

Most people I correspond with use the message format PGP/ MIME, and are annoyed when they have to read mail in inline format (the PGP Desktop default). To solve this problem, I can override the Opportunistic Encryption policy with my own and tell PGP to use PGP/MIME instead of inline format for all email that I can encrypt. To do so, I go into PGP Desktop's **PGP Messaging** section, choose **Edit Policies**, and then copy the existing Opportunistic Encryption policy to get a good starting point, as shown in Figure 9-4.

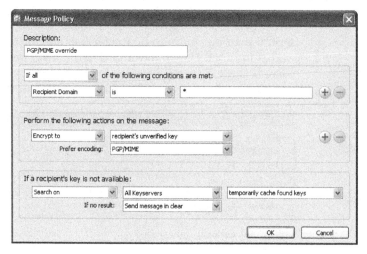

Figure 9-4: Setting the default message format to PGP/MIME

As you can see in Figure 9-4, I used the asterisk wildcard as the recipient domain; I did so to ensure that any mail sent anywhere matches this rule.

We encrypt by default, but note that the Prefer Encoding field says PGP/MIME, which becomes our new default. I could create similar rules to match the Require Encryption policy, but chances are that anyone relying on that policy is already using PGP Desktop and doesn't care what format the message arrives in.

Custom Policies Order and Disabling Policies

New policies are automatically placed at the top of the policy list under the assumption that you created these policies because you want them to take effect before any of the default policies!

This isn't always the case, however. For example, our second custom policy (the PGP/MIME override) matches any email sent anywhere, but we don't want messages to mailing lists to be either encrypted or signed. Therefore, this policy should go second to last, right above the Opportunistic Encryption policy. To put it there, go to the **PGP Messaging** portion of PGP Desktop and select **Edit Policy**, as shown in Figure 9-5.

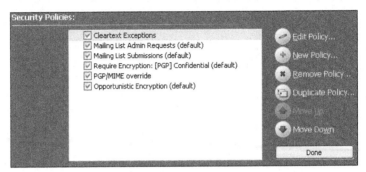

Figure 9-5: Editing PGP policies

Policies are processed in the order in which they appear in the Security Policies list, and the first policy that matches is used. In this example, the first custom policy, Cleartext Exceptions, is first, which means that any email address that matches this list should be sent unsigned and unencrypted, no matter what.

To entirely disable a policy, including any default policy you don't want, deselect the green checkbox next to that policy.

Notice that I moved the PGP/MIME override policy to be located next to last. As messages are handled according to the first matching policy, a policy that matches all possible messages would prevent any policies that appear beneath it from having any effect at all!

Policies give almost unlimited flexibility for managing email messages and ensure that your messages are processed consistently.

10

GNUPG AND EMAIL

Using GnuPG with email clients can be challenging because GnuPG is a command-line program, and today's most popular mail clients aren't. Still, if you spend a little time searching the Web, you can find GnuPG plug-ins for just about every popular mail client in mainstream use (although they will offer varying levels of functionality and usefulness).

This chapter will focus on integrating GnuPG with the three most popular Windows email clients: Microsoft Outlook Express, Microsoft Outlook, and Mozilla Thunderbird.

Microsoft Mail Clients and GnuPG

Because neither Outlook Express nor Outlook allow third-party software to access the raw MIME headers used by email, these programs don't work well with PGP/MIME mail. If, however, you correspond only with people who use inline encoding, Microsoft mail clients and GnuPG will work fine. You will have problems when people send you messages in PGP/MIME, however.

NOTE *Although the GnuPG team has a variety of clever ideas to make PGP/ MIME work anyway, as of this writing none of them is available for public consumption.*

Of course, you cannot control who sends you email, and many people use PGP/MIME. If you want to use free software and get sick of saying "I'm sorry, could you please resend your mail encrypted inline," I strongly encourage you to investigate the Thunderbird mail client. It is just as easy to use as either version of Outlook, it's free, it has more features, and it can import mail and accounts from Outlook Express. Nevertheless, we'll soldier on and push the Microsoft mail clients to their limits to see how well we can make them work.

NOTE *Before sending or reading OpenPGP email with either Outlook Express or Outlook, be sure to add your correspondent's public key to your WinPT keyring, as discussed in Chapter 7. The GnuPG plug-ins will generate scary-looking errors otherwise.*

Outlook Express and GnuPG

Outlook Express comes by default with Microsoft Windows, which makes it one of the most common low-end clients in the world. It meets most users' needs and is fairly simple to use.

GnuPG's Outlook Express plug-in comes bundled with WinPT. If the WinPT installer detects that you have Outlook Express on your computer, it should offer to install the plug-in for you. (Then again, if you followed the WinPT installation instructions in Chapter 4, you should already have the Outlook Express plug-in installed! If you didn't follow those instructions but want to use GnuPG with Outlook Express, reinstall WinPT.)

Configuring Outlook Express for OpenPGP

Because Outlook Express does not handle PGP/MIME, it won't read encrypted message content in anything but plain text. This means that you cannot encrypt fancy HTML messages. Before composing your secure messages in Outlook Express, configure the program as shown in Figure 10-1.

Figure 10-1: The Outlook Express Options Send tab

1. Go to the **Tools** menu and select **Options**.

2. On the Send tab, under Mail Sending Format, make sure that Plain Text is selected to ensure that Outlook Express will compose messages that will be compatible with inline encoding.

3. Make sure that Send Messages Immediately is *not* selected. If you try to sign or encrypt a message but fail (by making a typo on your passphrase, for example), when using immediate message sending, Outlook Express will send the message anyway—unsigned and unencrypted! Your message will cross the Net completely unprotected.

NOTE *Deselecting Send Messages Immediately means that you'll have to click the Send/Receive button to transmit your email instead of having Outlook Express just transmit when you're done writing the message. It also means that if your first attempt at encryption fails, you will have an opportunity to try again.*

Sending OpenPGP Mail

The GnuPG plug-in has no visible effect on Outlook Express until you click the Create Mail button. At this point, you should notice two additional options in your New Message screen, shown at the top right in Figure 10-2: Sign and Encrypt. (If you used Microsoft's proprietary digital signature system, you will probably recognize these buttons; the GnuPG plug-in authors simply recycled them.)

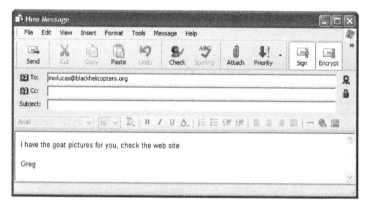

Figure 10-2: Composing Outlook Express mail with GnuPG

To sign your message, compose your message and click **Sign**. This makes a red ribbon appear to the right of the To: line. To encrypt and sign the message choose **Encrypt**, which will make a small blue lock symbol appear to the right of the Cc: line.

NOTE   *Note that this email message has no subject—we don't want anyone who intercepts the message to be able to glean any information about the message contents from the subject.*

When you click **Send**, GnuPG displays a dialog box asking you to enter your passphrase. Enter it, and your message is on its way!

Warnings and Caveats

You might see additional dialog boxes when trying to send your message using Outlook Express with GnuPG. For example, the plug-in might ask you to verify which public key you want to use for your recipient. If you have multiple private keys for your email address on your keyring, it will ask you to choose which key you wish to sign this message with.

Receiving and Verifying Signed and Encrypted Mail

When Outlook Express receives a inline-encoded OpenPGP message, the GnuPG plug-in intercepts the message and either automatically verifies the signature or requests your passphrase to decrypt the message. In either case, the results will be displayed in a pop-up window. The original message remains in its original form in Outlook Express.

When you receive a message that is in PGP/MIME format, reading it is quite difficult because, as you recall, Outlook Express does not give GnuPG access to the raw MIME headers necessary to decrypt messages within OE. (You can try to crack it open yourself, however, from the command line, as I discuss under "Decrypting PGP/MIME Messages with Microsoft Mail Clients" on page 145.)

Outlook and GnuPG

The German government sponsored the creation of a high-quality, freely available GnuPG plug-in for the Outlook program. This plug-in, called GPGol, is now maintained by g10code, a German firm that provides support for GnuPG and related software. (You can find links to the plug-in on g10code's website at www.g10code.com.) To use it, grab the most recent version of the Outlook plug-in, download it, and extract the files; then follow the installation instructions in the following section.

NOTE *The following instructions are for the version of GPGol available at press time. The limitations might be eliminated in the future, so be sure to check the documentation for the plug-in you download for updates!*

Installation

GPGol lacks a fancy installer, but installation is quite simple. The Zip file contains only two .dll files and a text file of instructions. Read the included instructions just to be sure that the process is unchanged, but for the past several releases the install process has been as follows:

1. Copy the .dll files to your Windows system directory (either C:\winnt\system32 or C:\windows\system32, depending on which version of Windows you're running).

2. Open a command prompt and type this:

```
C:> regsvr32 gpgol.dll
```

This will register the GnuPG/Outlook library with the operating system.

Configuring the Plug-In

Unlike the Outlook Express plug-in, the GnuPG plug-in does not require you to configure Outlook in any special way. If you make a typo when entering your passphrase, the Outlook GnuPG plug-in will let you try again rather than sending the message unencrypted, as with Outlook Express.

With the plug-in installed, restart Outlook, then go to the **Tools** menu and choose **Options**. You'll see a new tab called GnuPG, which allows you to configure your GnuPG settings. Before setting up GnuPG with Outlook, however, set Outlook to compose plaintext emails instead of fancy HTML text. Go to the **Mail Format** tab, as shown in Figure 10-3.

The first drop-down box under Mail Format allows you to set Outlook's default message format. Set this to **Plain Text**, as shown here. Not only will this make Outlook work well with GnuPG but it will also make your email more compatible with email from readers not using Microsoft software.

Now go to the GnuPG tab, as shown in Figure 10-4. The function of most of the settings should be obvious to you now (sign new messages by default, encrypt by default, and so on), but we'll discuss them briefly.

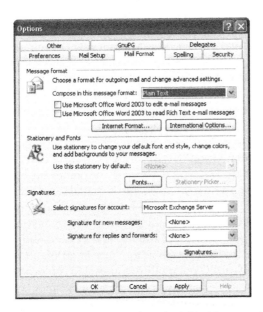

Figure 10-3: The Microsoft Outlook Mail Format tab configured for GnuPG

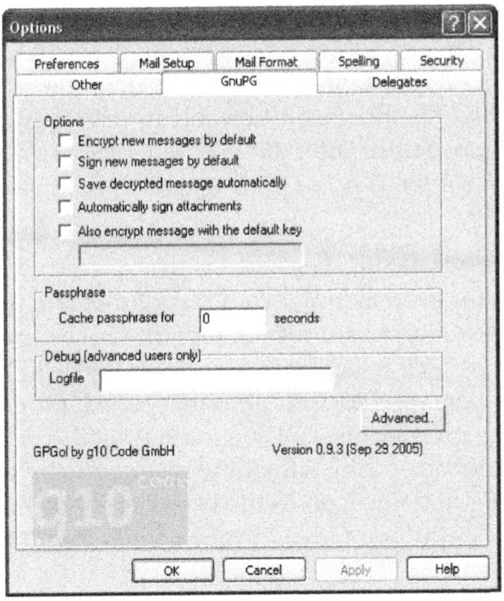

Figure 10-4: The Outlook GnuPG tab

Checkboxes

If you choose Encrypt New Messages By Default, any time you send an email Outlook will display a dialog box asking you to select the recipient's key. If you do not have the recipient's key in WinPT, you can cancel the encryption at sending time. Outlook will not automatically download keys upon request.

If you sign new messages by default, GnuPG will sign every email message you send, which will confuse people who have no idea what OpenPGP is.

The Save Decrypted Message Automatically option tells the plug-in to save the message in readable, plaintext form (as discussed in "Saving Email—Encrypted or Not?" on page 119) If you need to protect your documents even if your computer is stolen, definitely leave the messages encrypted.

The Also Encrypt Message With The Default Key option will make GnuPG encrypt every message you send with your public key as well as the recipient's (or recipients'). This means that you can use your passphrase to open mail that you have sent to someone else. This process might or might not fit in with your security requirements. For example, if you work in a dangerous area, being able to decrypt the messages you have sent might put your friends or coworkers at risk. However, if you're just an employee concerned about securing your documents in case your laptop is stolen on the subway, this might be a good idea. The thief won't be able to read these emails without your passphrase, after all. (We'll discuss this topic in more detail in Chapter 11.)

Passphrase

The plug-in can remember your passphrase after you type it, so if you have to work with several OpenPGP messages, you don't have to type your passphrase repeatedly. By default, the plug-in remembers your passphrase until you exit Outlook. (This is the setting for 0 seconds.) I suggest setting this to something like 120 seconds—long enough to give you some benefit, but not so long that if you go to the bathroom someone else can sit at your desk and send mail in your name without entering the passphrase.

Advanced

The Advanced tab lets you choose the path to the GnuPG and WinPT executables, as well as your keyring. You can use this to switch between multiple versions of GnuPG—say, if you're testing a new version but don't want to uninstall your old version yet.

Sending OpenPGP Mail

To send OpenPGP-encrypted mail from within Outlook:

1. Create a new mail message, just as you would without GnuPG.

2. Before you send the message, look under the Tools menu. You'll see three options: Encrypt Message While Sending, Sign Message While Sending, and Add Default Key To Message. The last option makes it easy to hand your public key to a new correspondent, whereas the first two sign or encrypt the message.

3. When you click **Send**, the plug-in will ask you for your passphrase. After you successfully enter it, Outlook will send your mail to the recipient.

If you include a plaintext attachment with your message, the plug-in will encrypt it separately, and the recipient will see it as a separate attachment.

NOTE *Remember, those attachments cannot be binary data such as images or documents; inline encoding works only with plain text!*

Receiving OpenPGP Mail

The Outlook GnuPG plug-in makes receiving inline-encoded OpenPGP mail from within Outlook very simple. When you click a message, GnuPG will display a message box requesting your passphrase. Enter it, and Outlook will display the message.

Encrypted documents will appear just like any other message; your only warning that they are encrypted is the passphrase dialog box. (Signed emails will have a header at the top that indicates whether the signature is valid or not.)

Decrypting PGP/MIME Messages with Microsoft Mail Clients

I've said all along that the GnuPG plug-ins for Microsoft mail clients don't speak PGP/MIME. You can work around this problem in a limited number of cases, however, by breaking out the GnuPG command line. (For details on GnuPG command-line operations, see Appendix B.)

All PGP/MIME messages arrive as attachments with the name msg.asc. If the encrypted message doesn't include attachments (that is, if the encrypted attachment doesn't include further subattachments), you might be able to decrypt it by hand. To do so:

1. Save msg.asc to your hard drive, open a command prompt, and go to the directory in which you have saved the file.

2. Use the --decrypt flag to gpg to decrypt a file. For example, this is what it would look like if my friend Greg decrypted a message I sent him (in response to an earlier email that he sent me):

```
c:> gpg --decrypt msg.asc

You need a passphrase to unlock the secret key for
user: "Greg E Donner  <gedonner@blackhelicopters.org>"
1792-bit ELG-E key, ID 80154DE0, created 2007-08-14 (main key ID 46CD08E9)❶

gpg: encrypted with 1792-bit ELG-E key, ID 80154DE0, created 2007-08-14
     "Greg E Donner (key #3) <gedonner@blackhelicopters.org>"
Content-Type: text/plain; charset=us-ascii
Content-Disposition: inline
Content-Transfer-Encoding: quoted-printable

Great, I'll get them to the paper right away!❷

gpg: Signature made 08/16/07 21:55:16  using DSA key ID E68C49BC
gpg: Good signature❸ from "Michael Warren Lucas Jr (Author, consultant,
sysadmin)
 <mwlucas@blackhelicopters.org>"
```

GnuPG immediately requests ❶ a passphrase to display ❷ the unencrypted message. Finally, the program tells you that the message's ❸ signature is valid.

Opening the message on the command line works easily only if there are no attachments in the original message. If the sender attached a document, you won't be able to crack it open this way.

NOTE *For a good summary of the GnuPG command line, see Appendix B.*

This is a lot of trouble to possibly read a PGP/MIME message, isn't it? This sort of thing is why using a different mail client (such as Thunderbird) is highly recommended, at least until the GnuPG folks figure out how to do PGP/MIME without all the pieces they currently need.[1]

---

[1] They'll get there, I'm sure of it. With my luck, it'll be about two weeks after this book hits the shelves.

Thunderbird and GnuPG

Thunderbird is the email component of the Mozilla application suite, a direct descendant of the Netscape web browser. The Mozilla Foundation produces several high-quality pieces of software, including the Firefox web browser, the Thunderbird mail client, the popular bug-tracking software Bugzilla, and so on. These tools are all free to end users. You can download Thunderbird at www.getthunderbird.org.

Thunderbird has rapidly been recognized as a high-quality mail suite and is a first choice among many people who need a powerful mail client. Because Thunderbird's source code is available for public use, the GnuPG developers have had no difficulties integrating all the features they desire into the plug-in.

Installing the Thunderbird GnuPG Plug-In

The Thunderbird GnuPG plug-in, Enigmail, is an extension that is installed into Thunderbird. (Thunderbird, like most Mozilla software, has an "extensions" framework to allow third-party developers to enhance the functionality of the main product.) Like Thunderbird itself, Enigmail is free.

To install the plug-in:

1. Download the plug-in from http://enigmail.mozdev.org and save it on your system. (If you're using the Mozilla web browser, Mozilla might think that Enigmail is a Mozilla plug-in, try to install it in the browser, and then complain that the installation fails because Enigmail is not compatible with Mozilla. Be sure to right-click and select **Save As** when downloading Enigmail.)

2. Start Thunderbird, open the **Tools** menu, and select **Extensions**. The Extensions panel will open.

3. Select **Install**, browse to where you saved Enigmail, and then double-click it. You will be asked to confirm that you want to install Enigmail. Say **Yes**.

4. After the install, restart Thunderbird, and you should see a new OpenPGP menu at the top of the main Thunderbird window.

Configuring Enigmail

To begin configuring Enigmail, choose **Enigmail ▶ Preferences** to bring up the configuration menu as shown in Figure 10-5.

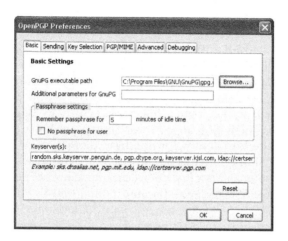

Figure 10-5: Enigmail Preferences

1. Your first step is to tell Enigmail where to find GnuPG by browsing to its program file, gpg.exe. (Remember, WinPT installs GnuPG under C:\Program Files\Windows Privacy Tools\GnuPG\gpg.exe.)

2. Like the other PGP plug-ins, Enigmail will cache your pass-phrase for a few minutes for you. The five-minute default is not unreasonable for most people, but I would err on the side of caution and reduce it to two or three minutes if you have a public or work computer. An hour might be reason-able for your home PC.

3. Enigmail provides a blank space to list your preferred keyservers in a comma-separated list, and it offers to fetch the necessary public keys when you receive a signed or encrypted message, using your preferred keyservers. Change the list of keyservers as needed to match your preferences.

4. Under Enigmail's Sending tab, as shown in Figure 10-6, are several options that control its basic functions. Perhaps the most important is the Encrypt To Self option, which saves a copy of your sent mail encrypted with your own key so you can access it later. (We discuss the advantages and disad-vantages of doing this in Chapter 8.)

Now enable Enigmail for the accounts you want to use it with. To do so:

1. Return to the **Tools** menu and select **Account Settings**.

2. In the pop-up window, select **OpenPGP Security**.

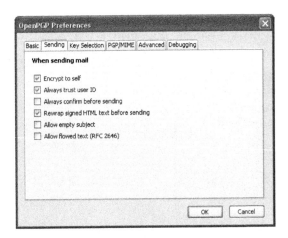

Figure 10-6: Enigmail sending options

3. Click the checkbox that says Enable OpenPGP Support (Enigmail) For This Identity to enable OpenPGP.

NOTE *By default, Enigmail will use the key with the user ID (UID) that matches the email address of the current account. For example, Greg's account is gedonner@blackhelicopters.org, so Enigmail looks for a keypair with that email address. To use a different key, specify the keyid here.*

4. From the **Account Settings** menu, select the **Composition & Addressing** section. Under Composition, turn off Compose Messages In HTML Format. (HTML messages can cause Enigmail problems.)

    Enigmail is now ready to use.

Sending OpenPGP Mail

To send mail using OpenPGP, click the **Write** button in Thunderbird's main window to open a new message. You should see an extra button at the top of the new message window that says *OpenPGP*. Select it, and Thunderbird will open a small dialog box that has three options, as shown in Figure 10-7.

Select **Sign Message** to sign this message. Select **Encrypt Message** to encrypt the message. While Enigmail defaults to using inline encoding, Enigmail will let you use either inline or PGP/MIME encoding, so you can work around any restrictions that your recipients might have. Those friends of yours who are stuck using Outlook with GnuPG won't have to jump through hoops to converse with you, while you'll also be able to communicate with people using PGP/MIME, email attachments, and so on.

Figure 10-7: Thunderbird/
Enigmail mail-sending options

Per-Recipient Rules

Although Thunderbird provides all this flexibility, your brain probably isn't up to coping with it. (Mine sure isn't!) How can you possibly remember how each person you correspond with can most easily read OpenPGP mail? Enigmail lets you create rules for each of your correspondents. When you define a rule for a correspondent, each time you send them a message Enigmail will process it according to that rule.

To define a rule:

1. Choose the **Enigmail** menu from the main Thunderbird screen, then select **Edit Per-Recipient Rules**. A window appears, listing all your rules for recipients. Figure 10-8 shows the Per-Recipient Rules Editor with a single rule.

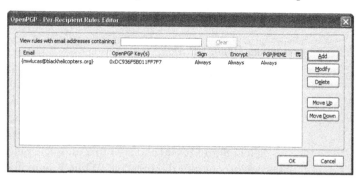

Figure 10-8: The Per-Recipient Rules Editor

2. Select **Add** to create a new rule, such as the one I created in Figure 10-9.

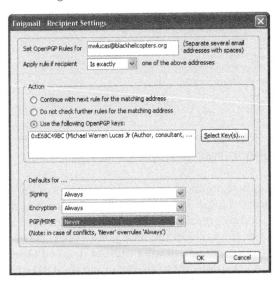

Figure 10-9: Per-recipient rule creation

Here, I created a rule for any email sent to my email address: mwlucas@blackhelicopters.org. I chose a particular OpenPGP key to use when corresponding with this address and chose to sign and encrypt by default every message sent to this address. The PGP/MIME option saves me the trouble of remembering whether this recipient can read PGP/MIME or must receive inline-encoded mail; in this case, it's set to Never. The next time a message is sent to mwlucas@blackhelicopters .org, Enigmail will automatically encrypt and/or sign it as the rule dictates and encode it properly for this recipient.

The Per-Recipient Rules allow you to create rules that match entire domains, particular usernames, or just about anything you like.

Reading OpenPGP Mail

Enigmail does an excellent job of handling OpenPGP mail in both inline or PGP/MIME format. When you attempt to open an OpenPGP message, Enigmail will display a dialog box and request your passphrase. It couldn't be easier.

Enigmail also provides an excellent view of the message's OpenPGP status, as shown in Figure 10-10.

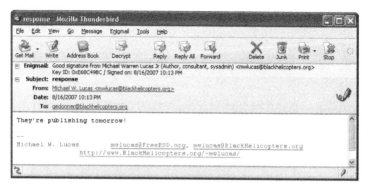

Figure 10-10: Reading an OpenPGP message

In the Enigmail area, we see the status of the OpenPGP signature. Enigmail has verified the signature of this email, as indicated by green coloration, and the signature is described as Good. If you select the blue pen to the right of the message information, Enigmail will print out detailed OpenPGP information about this message, including the UID of the sender's key, the date the message was signed, and the fingerprint of the signing key. If the signature is bad, the pen icon on the right side of the header will appear as a broken pen.

Upgrading Thunderbird and Enigmail

The Thunderbird and Enigmail developers release new versions of their software fairly regularly, and upgrading Enigmail without updating Thunderbird is very simple. In fact, the Thunderbird Extensions Manager will actually check to see whether new versions of Enigmail are available and offer to upgrade for you.

If you upgrade Thunderbird, however, things get a little trickier. Before upgrading Thunderbird, you should be sure to uninstall Enigmail. However, uninstalling is, unfortunately, not enough to completely eradicate Enigmail's leftovers.

Both Enigmail and Thunderbird store configurations and settings in a profile directory. When you upgrade Thunderbird, the new version will use the same profile directory, so you can retain your saved passwords and other settings between upgrades. However, an Enigmail configuration for an old Thunderbird install will only confuse the new Thunderbird and generally cause any of a wide variety of confusing and obscure errors.

To avoid this problem, find your Thunderbird profile directory, which is in the user's application data directory (usually C:\Documents and Settings*username*\Application Da Thunderbird). You'll find a Profiles directory here. In that directory, you'll find a directory with a name made of eight random characters and a .default extension. This is where Enigmail stores its information.

After uninstalling Enigmail, but before upgrading Thunderbird, delete the following from your profile directory:

- XUL.mfl

- Everything in the chrome directory

Now upgrade Thunderbird and reinstall Enigmail. You should be ready to go again!

You now know how to use GnuPG with the most popular mail clients. To round things off, let's look at some of the other things you should be aware of when using OpenPGP.

11

OTHER OPENPGP CONSIDERATIONS

You should now have a decent understanding of how to use OpenPGP with PGP and GnuPG, and should be able to quickly comprehend any other OpenPGP products. To round things off, let's consider some other points to remember when working with OpenPGP, PGP, and GnuPG. Because no security protocol is perfect, we'll discuss what can go wrong with OpenPGP. We'll discuss some concerns about the interoperability of PGP and GnuPG (as well as other OpenPGP programs) and how groups of people can share a single key, with minimal risk. Finally, we'll discuss a few ways to make OpenPGP use on a shared system slightly less intolerable, and end with a discussion of some of the extra features found in WinPT and PGP.

What Can Go Wrong?

Although OpenPGP provides a reliable method of proving message authenticity, note that the acronym *PGP* stands for *Pretty Good Privacy*. It doesn't stand for Perfectly Grand Privacy, let alone Penultimate Guaranteed Privacy. *Pretty Good* means exactly that—it's better than what existed before, but it isn't unbreakable. Mallory (any bad guy; see Chapter 1) has many methods to break OpenPGP's protections. Most of the methods Mallory can use to violate someone's privacy play off a victim's ignorance. Remember the finer points of OpenPGP usage (as discussed following), and you'll frustrate Mallory so much that he'll give up and go bother someone else.

Poor Usage

By far, the most common way that OpenPGP is weakened is when it's not correctly used. Incorrect OpenPGP usage creates the appearance of security, but actually creates an insecure situation. The appearance of security is worse than no security; if my front door looks locked but isn't, I'd like to know.

Poor usage can be anything that doesn't comply with the rules of OpenPGP. If you leave your private key on your website, even in a hidden directory, it will be found. "Beam me up, Scotty!" is not a passphrase; it's an invitation to identity theft. And emailing your passphrase and private key to yourself "so you won't lose it" is just daft. I've seen people make all these mistakes (to their eventual dismay).

The usual reason that people give for not using OpenPGP properly is that it's complicated. That's true; it is complicated. Privacy and security as a whole are not easy, but if you're reading this book you've obviously decided that they're worth some effort to preserve.

Some people even go so far as to keep their OpenPGP keys on a computer that isn't connected to the network. Anything that they sign or encrypt is placed on removable media, moved to that computer, processed with OpenPGP, and returned to the networked computer. This is probably too extreme for most people, but it is very viable if your security requirements demand that level of protection and it adds a nice layer of physical security that is very hard to break.

Poor Signing

Let's consider poor signing. "This guy says he's Michael W. Lucas; I'll trust him." BZZZZT! I'm sorry, please play again.

When you sign someone's key, you are not only validating that person's identity for your own use but you are also publicly affirming that you have verified the person's identity. A person who tricks someone else into signing a key generated for a fraudulent identity can successfully hook into the Web of Trust and gain the confidence of others.

Remember, you *can* use someone else's public key without signing it. If I were to send you email, you could import my public key and use it to read mail encrypted with the matching private key. You would have no guarantee that I was who I claimed to be, but you would have a guarantee that any further correspondence signed with the same key came from a person who had access to the same private key.

Hardware Compromise

If someone has physical access to your computer, he can get your passphrase. Hardware-based keystroke loggers that plug into your keyboard cable and record everything you type are available online for less than $100.

Some hardware-based keystroke loggers are small enough to fit inside a laptop. Mallory could sneakily attach the logger to your system while you're at lunch, wait a few days, and then unplug the device from your machine and see everything you typed. If you typed your passphrase during that time, he has it. Wading through everything you typed could be a lot of work, but if Mallory is sufficiently motivated, he'll do it.

NOTE *Both police and private investigators routinely use keystroke loggers. If you are actually at risk of such an investigation, be sure to check your hardware for keystroke loggers before using OpenPGP. Even using an alternate keyboard layout is no defense against a hardware keystroke logger;[1] after Mallory figures out that nothing you typed makes any sense, he'll have the analysis software unscramble the letters.*

You can work around this problem by using a "software" or "virtual" keyboard. These programs display a keyboard on the monitor, which you use by selecting characters with the mouse. This is for the very careful, to be sure, but if you're at risk of keyboard logging you will be glad you have it. But remember: Even though a virtual keyboard is clumsy to use, don't make

---

[1] On the other hand, a Dvorak keyboard layout is an excellent defense against people borrowing your computer during lunch. I highly recommend it for this purpose, if for no other reason.

your passphrase shorter just for convenience; the whole reason you're using it is to protect that vital passphrase!

Although we concentrated on passphrase theft, the file containing your private key is just as important as the passphrase itself. If someone has physical access to your machine, the person can always break open the case and steal or copy your hard drive to get your private key file. For this reason, many people keep all their public and private keys on a USB flash drive: It's more difficult for someone to steal your cryptographic keys if they're kept with your car keys or in your watch.

Software Compromise

If your operating system is insecure, Mallory can violate your privacy from almost anywhere in the world. Worms, viruses, and spyware can all gather your keystrokes just like a hardware keystroke logger, with the added advantage of not requiring physical access to your machine. Some spyware actively searches out passwords and passphrases, whereas other viruses give administrative control of your machine to someone else.

This problem is fairly simple to defend against.

- First, keep your machine fully patched. If you're a Windows user, sprinkle Microsoft Update generously over your system on a regular basis.

- Macintosh, Linux, and BSD users should apply security patches as soon as they are available.

- Install antivirus software, update it regularly, and use it continuously.

- Keep your OpenPGP software up to date.

No vendor has a perfect security record, and security patches don't solve everything, but most electronic crimes are crimes of opportunity; criminals choose the easiest targets. Applying the proper patches will make you a more difficult target, however, and make Mallory more likely to attack someone else. (Like the Club you put on the steering wheel of your car, it's not perfect but it sure makes it hard to turn the wheel unless you can remove it.)

Also, if you have a broadband connection, either turn your PC off when not in use or get a hardware firewall. Years ago when broadband first came out, many tech-savvy people said, "Leave your computer on all the time; it'll be fine." Today, criminals make fortunes every month turning thousands of infected, always-on PCs into potent weapons. If someone can use your computer as part of a swarm to bring down an e-commerce site, they can certainly pull your passphrases and passwords out of it as well. (And, as one of these "tech-savvy" people who used to recommend leaving your computer on, I officially request permission to eat my words. With a nice side helping of crow.)

If you are seriously concerned about the security of your system, I encourage you to get a book on the topic. Too much security is better than not enough.

People Compromise

The best way for Mallory to penetrate OpenPGP's protections is to get your passphrase and private key file. Stealing the file containing your private key requires compromising your machine, which proper system security will make difficult. Mallory needs to get you to give him the passphrase in some manner, though, and that's where you make his work difficult. If you are using OpenPGP correctly, that passphrase resides only in your head. Mallory's problem lies in extracting the passphrase from your head. If he isn't subtle, Mallory can just arrange for goons with iron pipes to beat it out of you. This risk is so common in certain situations that the encryption community calls it "rubber hose cryptanalysis."[2]

Quite a few people take the mere presence of an Open-PGP signature as proof of authenticity. This leads to a whole variety of attacks similar to the "phishing" emails used to try to trick people out of their bank account numbers. These attacks don't go after OpenPGP itself, but they leverage OpenPGP to create an illusion of security. To give this appearance, all Mallory has to do is find a real OpenPGP signature in a mailing list archive or on Usenet and attach that signature to an email. Many people won't bother to verify that signature, assuming that nobody would have the sheer bravado to fake a signature. Similarly, once Mallory has compromised someone else's email account, he might upload an OpenPGP key for that person to several public keyservers. He could then pose as that person with impunity. Mallory might also upload several keys for a different person to a keyserver, in the hope that his victim would choose one of those keys as legitimate or might even hunt for a key that can read a message without understanding the implications of his actions. Security experts are discussing ways to make these attacks more difficult to execute, but no changes

---

[2] For the record, anyone with a weapon and the proper attitude can have my passphrase upon request.

to the OpenPGP infrastructure can protect a genuinely gullible person.

There's also legal action, which is more interesting. Cryptography laws vary greatly from country, but here's the status under current US law.

Under US case law, a court can subpoena anything that is written down, including passphrases. Mallory only has to persuade a judge that he should issue a court order for your written passphrase. If you have memorized your key (as you should), precedent has not yet been established, but it's fairly certain that you can at least be found in contempt of court for refusing to disclose your passphrase.

One idea that has been batted about repeatedly is that of applying Fifth Amendment protections to passphrases. If you have encrypted documents wherein you have recorded that you have committed a crime, shouldn't the right to not incriminate yourself apply? The law considers a passphrase more like a key for a safe deposit box; the key is not protected, although documents in the deposit box might be. Therefore, the Fifth Amendment does not apply to passphrases as such.

An interesting twist on this idea is to have your passphrase include a criminal confession, the more horrendous and detailed the better. Although the court can require you to turn over a passphrase, the Fifth Amendment might apply if your passphrase is this: "On March 8, 2005, I slaughtered 16 nuns, burned an American flag, and psychologically abused a poodle in Moosebane, Idaho." The problem here is that you must have actually committed the crime—the Fifth Amendment certainly does not apply to things you haven't done! This has not been tested in court but, sadly, I expect it will be before long.

The law is similar in many other countries. For example, the British Association of Chief Police Officers is attempting to get legislation that would make withholding decryption keys a crime.

The bottom line is this: Ask before you get yourself into trouble! I would hate to see a reader get thrown into a Third World prison for violating local cryptography laws. In countries where owning this book is illegal and the law is enforced by truncheon-bearing goons, you will even want to ask the question quietly. OpenPGP is great for protecting yourself from privacy violations by other civilians and for notifying you when the government is violating your privacy. Once the gears of justice begin grinding, however, its protections drop.

Fake Keys

Because anyone can create an OpenPGP public key with anyone's name on it, annoying twits occasionally upload keys in other people's names. For example, if I search subkeys.pgp.net for "George W. Bush" I find no fewer than seven keys with that name. Several are for the email address president@whitehouse.gov. If George W. used OpenPGP, we'd all have a hard time sorting out which key was his.

The PGP Corporation's keyserver avoids this problem by requiring a response from the email address owner before making the key public. I suspect that more and more keyserver networks will adopt this approach, but that's for the future.

The moral of this story is this: If you find several keys for one person, check their signatures. A key that is tightly integrated into the Web of Trust is much more likely to be valid than one that has few or no signatures. In this example, none of the George W. Bush keys has any signatures. Presumably, the President of the United States would be able to find at least one person who could confirm his identity and sign his key. People who are actually named George W. Bush, but with different email addresses, have keys signed by other people.

Also, check alternative public key sources such as the person's home page. Should the President ever start using OpenPGP, it's a pretty safe bet that his public key will be available somewhere on www.whitehouse.gov! (I'm sure that the US President has some sort of email encryption available, but it's either not OpenPGP or not hooked into the Web of Trust.)

Ultimately, the only way to verify any OpenPGP key is through the Web of Trust, but only you can decide who to trust and how far to trust them.

OpenPGP Interoperability

The OpenPGP standard insists that all OpenPGP programs be able to use the SHA-1 hash and 3DES encryption, but allows implementers to offer additional methods if they desire. OpenPGP vendors have a wide choice of specific implementation methods and don't always choose the same hash and encryption algorithms. Too, different versions of OpenPGP programs might prefer to use different algorithms. Generally speaking, the best way to ensure that your software can communicate with any other OpenPGP software is to install all the algorithms and hash methods available. Some of these hashes are insecure, and could be forged—particularly MD5, and to a lesser extent SHA-1. People who use these are not as secure as they believe, but you can choose to communicate with them if you wish.

This still leaves the problem of pre-OpenPGP versions of PGP that don't use 3DES. These older versions almost always have security problems, and older versions of the OpenPGP specification have security problems of their own. People using PGP version 2 should upgrade. Feel free to assume that messages sent with PGP version 2 are insecure—because they are.

NOTE *If you truly want your communications to be secure, help other people upgrade their software rather than communicating with them via their old vulnerable tools. People who use this older software are fooling themselves if they believe it is secure. Remember, the appearance of security is worse than no security!*

Teams and OpenPGP

Many companies have a team of people who sign files. For example, many pieces of software you find on the Internet have an OpenPGP signature. Several people on the development team know the passphrase. This is reasonable if not ideal, provided that the key's UID clearly labels it as a team key; the trick here is in knowing when to change the key.

A common misconception is that when someone leaves the team, you can secure the key by changing the passphrase. There's a problem here, though: What if the person who departed has a copy of the private key with the old passphrase? OpenPGP keys don't come with labels that shout "Now with new, improved passphrase!" The departed person can use the old passphrase with his copy of the private key to sign as many documents as he desires, and nobody will know the difference.

When you use a team key and have a personnel change, the only safe action is to immediately revoke the old key, make the revoked key available, and generate a new keypair. When you put the revoked key out on the keyserver, everyone who updates a key will get the revocation notice.

NOTE *Although OpenPGP software decrypts email messages encrypted with a revoked key, it does not encrypt messages with a revoked key.*

OpenPGP and Shared Systems

Throughout this book I've pounded home the idea that your OpenPGP computer should be a single-user system, but you might choose to make an exception. For example, corporate computers frequently have an administrative team that handles OS updates, antivirus protection, and so on, and these people have administrative access to all the computers in the company. If you must use OpenPGP in such an environment, here are some ways to mitigate the risk:

- If you're using Windows 95, Windows 98, or Windows Me and cannot upgrade to a more modern operating system, give up. Anyone who can turn your machine on can get your private key. These operating systems are simply not secure, period, end.

- For Windows NT–based and Unix-like operating systems, set the permissions on your keyring files so that nobody but you can read them. Windows permissions are quite useful in this case—the system administrator can change the permissions on your keyring only by taking ownership of the directory, a fairly obvious hint that your keyring has been compromised. Many Unix-like operating systems support Mandatory Access Controls (MAC), which have similar effects.

- You can protect your keyring even more by keeping it on a USB flash drive or other small portable storage device. Most keyrings will fit 20 times over on a floppy disk (if your computer even has a floppy drive). Various firms have recently started making OpenPGP "smartcards," where the entire key stays on the card. These add a whole new layer of security to OpenPGP, even on a shared system.

- If you must copy your keys to the local hard drive, install a program to thoroughly delete them when you're finished. A Google search for "secure delete" will turn up dozens of freely available secure deletion programs. PGP includes one, as we discuss on the next page.

- When using GnuPG on a Windows system shared by several people, consider creating a folder named C:\GnuPG and copying the GnuPG program files to it; then add that directory to the system's PATH variable. Every user will then have access to that same version of GnuPG, which will at least eliminate the problems that arise from people using different versions of the program.

- If you don't entirely trust your machine at work, consider creating two OpenPGP keys: one for work and one for home. Sign your work key with your personal key. Never bring your personal key to work; instead, have people sign your personal key and sign others' keys with your personal key.

NOTE *Your work key is ultimately disposable—you will probably have several jobs during your lifetime but only one reputation. And keep a revocation certificate at home in case your company elects to show you the door without notice. (I do not place my work keys on a keyserver; I distribute them privately and only to correspondents who absolutely require it.)*

Although these actions won't protect you from a malicious systems administrator, they can reduce the damage and make living with such a setup a little more tolerable. As a long-time systems administrator, I can assure you that most sysadmins would never mess with a user's OpenPGP keys. That's not because we're inherently trustworthy, but rather because any sysadmin who gets his kicks by violating others' privacy quickly annoys the wrong person and gets fired. After this happens a couple of times, their reputation is in a shambles and they're unemployable in the computer field. You're under much greater risk from other users of the computer.

Despite any precautions, physical access trumps all. If someone can open your computer and walk off with your hard drive, it's all over. Hopefully, you chose a good strong passphrase to protect your private key against this risk!

Other Software Features

Both WinPT and PGP offer special features that will be of use to people interested in privacy. Although these features are not part of OpenPGP, they rate a mention.

Passphrase Caching

Both sets of software will cache your passphrase for a user-configurable length of time, which will save you a bit of typing. However, when you use this option, if you step away from the machine, anyone who sits down can use your OpenPGP software because your passphrase is still cached. I suggest setting this time to only a few minutes, or manually flushing your passphrase before you leave your desk.

Shredding

"Shredding" is another add-on feature in both WinPT and PGP. When you delete a document from a computer via the operating system, it isn't destroyed. Much as if you put a print-out in the trash, the document is merely hidden from view and set on a path that will lead to its eventual destruction.

Any number of programs can recover these deleted files. To permanently and irrevocably destroy a file, use the shredder function that ships with PGP and WinPT. These programs overwrite the file on disk several times, eliminating any hope of recovering it. (If you're using an operating system that has filesystem journaling, shredding is certainly less effective, but it will raise the bar for recovery.)

If you want real security, shred any earlier versions of the file because previous drafts might be just as incriminating as the shredded version. If it's that important to destroy a document, be sure to check for any backups.

Winston Churchill told a story about a man who received a telegram informing him that his mother-in-law had passed and asking what sort of funeral arrangements he desired. The man replied "Embalm. Cremate. Bury at sea. Take no chances!" This is a good model for electronic document destruction.

PGP Desktop also offers the ability to encrypt your instant messages, which goes a long way toward making IM useful in a business environment. It can also encrypt your whole disk drive, giving excellent protection against data loss in case of laptop theft (although doing so will add a significant amount of overhead).

Experiment with your chosen software; you'll find it has abilities far beyond what we covered in this book and uses far beyond what you thought you needed.

Enjoy and protect your privacy!

A

INTRODUCTION TO PGP COMMAND LINE

 In addition to PGP Desktop, PGP Corporation produces a command-line PGP program, PGP Command Line, which allows you to automate PGP operations. PGP Command Line is a licensed product that has many features required by enterprise customers. It is available for Windows and a variety of Unix-like operating systems (including Mac OS X). It comes with a very good and complete manual (over 300 pages) and can easily be installed by any systems administrator who has read this book.

This appendix will introduce you to the basic PGP Command Line functions. We'll cover the basics very quickly so that you can handle simple PGP Command Line operations in short order. (Read the manual for more detail on the PGP Command Line's various commands and reference this book for detail on specific suggestions.) We are specifically not covering functionality such as Additional Decryption Keys, which are well documented in the manual but require in-depth explanation.

PGP Command Line runs the same way on Windows and Unix-like operating systems; the only difference is the appearance of the command prompt. We'll use a hash mark (#) as a prompt in the examples here, as some Unix shells do. Users with normal privileges can use PGP Command Line just fine.

NOTE *Unlike most command-line programs, PGP Command Line does not interact with the user after execution begins. It is designed for automated environments in which there is no user to talk to and it does not prompt you for further information. This is quite useful behavior for scripts, of course.*

PGP Command Line Configuration

All PGP Command Line configuration, key storage, and other information is kept in an application data directory. If you're using Windows, you'll set the location of this directory during the install; if you're on a Unix-like system, that directory will be $HOME/.pgp. To change PGP Command Line's behavior, you edit the configuration file PGPprefs.xml. The defaults are suitable for almost all applications, but you'll find a full explanation of the variables in the PGP Command Line manual.

The configuration file must use valid XML for PGP Command Line to work. Fortunately, this isn't difficult; each entry looks something like this:

```
<key>CLpassphraseCacheTimeout</key>❶
<integer>120</integer>❷
```

In this example, the variable ❶ CLpassphraseCacheTimeout, which controls the length of time that your passphrase is cached, has been set to ❷ 120. To change this timeout value, edit the 120 without altering the surrounding tags.

The files pubring.pkr and secring.skr are two additional important files in this directory. Your public keyring is stored in pubring.pkr, whereas your private keys are stored in secring .skr. Guard secring.skr very carefully, for reasons I hope have been sufficiently driven home by the time you've read this far!

NOTE *When editing a configuration file like this one, it's very easy to acciden-
tally delete an angle bracket without noticing and break the software
as a result. Therefore, keep a backup of your known-good configuration file! It's much easier to fall back to a good version and try again
than to stare at a broken configuration for hours trying to find what
you missed before. If you're on a Unix-like operating system, I strongly
recommend using the RCS revision control system for managing configuration files. It's been used for decades so most of the bugs are gone,
and it's free.*

Testing and Licensing

After you finish installing PGP Command Line, make sure
that it works by trying the --version and --help options. The
--version option displays the version of PGP Command Line
you have, whereas --help displays all the options and flags that
PGP Command Line uses. If these options work, your installation is correct.

After you know that the base install is correct, you should
license the software; if your install is not licensed, PGP Command Line (PGPCL) functions only in a very limited manner.
You must have Internet access to license PGP Command Line
because the program contacts the PGP license server and confirms that your license code matches your name, email address,
and organization. You must enter your name, organization,
email address, and license code exactly as they appear in the
license or the license operation will fail. For example:

```
# pgp --license-authorize❶ --license-name "Michael Lucas"❷ --license-
organization "Author (Press)"❸ --license-number "long-string-of-codes"❹
--license-email "mwlucas@blackhelicopters.org"❺
```

Here we tell PGPCL to ❶ authorize the license that PGP
Corporation has on file for ❷ the license owner and ❸ the
organization the license owner belongs to, using ❹ the license
code provided by PGP Corporation and ❺ the email address
of the license owner. This process will make PGPCL contact
the PGP Corporation's licensing server and verify your information. If you entered all the information correctly and the
license is valid, PGP Command Line will add licensing information to PGPprefs.xml, and you'll be ready to go!

Creating a Keypair

PGP Command Line creates many different sorts of keypairs in addition to the standard OpenPGP signing and encryption keys. The format for creating an OpenPGP keypair is as follows, where ❶ *UID* is a standard PGP user ID, consisting of a name followed by an email address in angle brackets:

```
# pgp --gen-key "UID"❶ --key-type rsa❷ --encryption-bits 2048❸
--passphrase "passphrase"❹ --other-options
```

To use an optional comment, as discussed in Chapter 2, add it between the name and the email address in parentheses. (PGP will emit a warning about this being nonstandard, but many people have UIDs in exactly that format, and they work just fine.) For example, my UID is this:

```
Michael Warren Lucas Jr (Author, consultant, sysadmin) <mwlucas@
blackhelicopters.org>
```

This UID differentiates me from every other OpenPGP-using Michael Lucas in the world.

PGP Command Line supports several different ❷ types of keypairs. (If you're into cryptography or have specific business needs for signing-only keys or the like, see the manual for details because we'll cover only OpenPGP keypairs.)

Setting the Key Type

Modern OpenPGP keys are of type RSA. You set the type of key with the --key-type flag.

You can choose ❸ the number of bits in the keypair (as discussed in Chapter 1), which ranges from 1024 to 4096. I suggest using 2048, which as of this writing should protect your data for the next several years.

Assigning a Passphrase

You must give your ❹ passphrase on the command line when you create your key. If you don't want to assign a passphrase when you create this key, you can change it later with the --change-passphrase option.

Setting an Expiration Date

By default, new keys have no expiration date. To set an expiration date, use the optional --expiration-date flag, with the date in YYYY-MM-DD format, such as 2008-12-31.

For example, to create a keypair for myself, I would run the following:

```
# pgp --gen-key "Michael Warren Lucas Jr (Consultant, author, sysadmin)
<mwlucas@blackhelicopters.org>" --key-type rsa --encryption-bits 2048 --
passphrase "This is a really bad passphrase" --expiration-date 2008-12-31
```

PGP will quickly generate a key and end by listing the keyid.

Generating Revocation Certificates

As with any other OpenPGP key, it's important to create a revocation certificate immediately upon certificate creation. To create a revocation certificate, use the --gen-revocation command like so:

```
# pgp --gen-revocation "UID"❶ --passphrase "passphrase"❷
--force❸
```

The first argument tells PGP Command Line which key to revoke. You need only enough of ❶ the UID to uniquely identify a key on your keyring. For example, my keyring has only one key on it with the email address mwlucas@blackhelicopters .org. That email address uniquely identifies my key on my keyring. If I had several keys with that email address, I would need to use a larger part of the UID to identify the key I wanted to revoke, or perhaps the complete UID if I had several very similar keys.

Next, give your ❷ passphrase on the command line.

Finally, use ❸ the --force flag to tell PGP, "Yes, I know this isn't normal, but you won't ask me if I'm sure, so I'm telling you yes, I'm sure; I really do want you to do it."

For example, to create a revocation certificate for my key, I would type this:

```
# pgp --gen-revocation mwlucas@blackhelicopters.org --passphrase
"This is a really bad passphrase" --force
```

PGP Command Line will create a revocation certificate and place it in the current directory in a file named after my complete UID. (Save and protect this certificate, as discussed in Chapter 2.)

Exporting Your Public Key

Next you'll need to distribute your public key to your correspondents, either by using keyservers or text files.

Distributing to Keyservers

Send your public key to a keyserver with the --keyserver-send option, and use the --keyserver option to choose the keyserver:

```
# pgp --keyserver-send UID --keyserver protocol://keyserver
```

The UID is either the whole UID of the key we want to publicize or a large enough piece of it so that PGP can identify it.

The keyserver must include the protocol used to access the keyserver and the keyserver's name. Common protocols include LDAP (used by PGP Corporation's keyserver) and HTTP (used by keyservers such as subkeys.pgp.net). Include the protocol before the machine name, much like a URL. For example, to send my newly generated PGP key to the PGP Corporation's keyserver, keyserver.pgp.com, I would run this:

```
# pgp --keyserver-send mwlucas@blackhelicopters.org --keyserver
ldap://keyserver.pgp.com
```

By default, PGP Command Line will contact the PGP Corporation's public keyserver. You only need the --keyserver flag if you want to contact a different keyserver.

Exporting to Text Files

Use the --export command to pull your public key from your keyring into a text file:

```
# pgp --export UID
```

This command will create a text file with the same name as your UID. If you've already created a revocation certificate and haven't renamed it, PGP Command Line will complain that it can't create the file. If that's the case, rename your revocation certificate and export the key again.

Viewing Keys

To see all the keys on your keyring, use the --list-keys option. Or to view a particular key on your keyring, list the UID or a portion thereof after --list-keys; PGP Command Line will only list keys that have the given string in the UID.

For example, here's how you'd search for all keys on the keyring that include the string mwlucas.

```
# pgp --list-keys mwlucas
 Alg  Type Size/Type Flags   Key ID     User ID
 ----- ---- --------- ------- ---------- -------
*RSA4 pair 2048/2048 [VI---] 0x7E02501C Michael Warren Lucas Jr
(Consultant, author, sysadmin) <mwlucas@blackhelicopters.org>
1 key found
#
```

PGP Command Line found one matching key (big surprise, I know). (This becomes much more useful after we add keys to the keyring, as shown later in this appendix.)

The default view is very brief, but you can view any level of detail about this key with the options shown in Table A-1 (just give the option and a UID or unique portion thereof).

Table A-1: PGP Command Line Key Viewing Options

Option	Function
--pgp-fingerprint	Displays the fingerprint of the specified key
--list-key-details	Shows all information included in the key
--list-sigs	Shows all signatures on the key
--list-sig-details	Shows detailed information about all signatures
--list-userids	Shows all UIDs included in this key

For example, to view all the signatures on my key, I would run the following:

```
# pgp --list-sigs mwlucas@blackhelicopters.org
```

Managing PGP Command Line Keyrings

Keyservers are most commonly used to search for keys, add keys to your keyring, sign keys, and update keys.

Searching for Keys

To use PGP Command Line to find someone's key on a keyserver, you need the UID (or a portion thereof) and the name of the keyserver you want to search.

The best way to search for a key is to use the user's email address. Here, we search subkeys.pgp.net for any key with the string Michael Lucas.[1]

```
# pgp --keyserver-search "Michael Lucas" --keyserver http://subkeys.pgp.net
http://subkeys.pgp.net:keyserver search (2504:successful search)
 Alg  Type Size/Type Flags   Key ID      User ID
 ----- ---- --------- ------- ---------- -------
 DSS  pub  2048/1024 [-----] 0xE68C49BC Michael Warren Lucas Jr (Author, consul-
tant, sysadmin) <mwlucas@blackhelicopters.org>❶
 DSS  pub  2048/1024 [-----] 0xAB6CA178 Michael Lucas <mike.lucas@teamlucas.com>
 DSS  pub  2048/1024 [-----] 0x4922B639 Michael P. Lucas <mlucas@jharris.com>
 DSS  pub  2048/1024 [-----] 0x4768326E B. Michael Lucas <n1tba@snet.net>
 DSS  pub  2048/1024 [-----] 0xAD08B0C7 David Michael Lucas <trajan97@yahoo.com>
 DSS  pub  2048/1024 [-----] 0xFB31770D David Michael Lucas <Buckeye_D@yahoo.com>
6 keys found
```

The keyserver reports that it has six keys that match the string Michael Lucas and presents the results, but I'm only interested in one of them. Fortunately, the list includes ❶ the UID of all the keys so I can see which key I want and then use a unique portion of the UID to import it.

Importing Keys

Use the --keyserver-recv option to download a public key from a keyserver and add it to your public keyring:

```
# pgp --keyserver-recv mwlucas@blackhelicopters.org --keyserver
http://subkeys.pgp.net
```

PGP will download the key and add it to your keyring, making it permanently available locally.

Signing a Key

After you have examined a key's fingerprint and UID and inspected the key owner's identification (as discussed in Chapter 5), you might choose to sign the key.

PGP Command Line allows you to specify several types of signature; we'll discuss the old-fashioned exportable signature

---

[1] I'm using the pgp.net keyserver instead of the official PGP Corporation keyserver to illustrate a point; my keys are available on both subkeys.pgp.net and keyserver.pgp.com, but the results from the PGP Corporation keyserver are boringly correct thanks to their email verification process.

used to build the Web of Trust. The format of a signature is as follows:

```
# pgp --sign-key UID-of-key-to-be-signed❶ --signer your-UID❷
--sig-type exportable --passphrase passphrase❸
```

You must tell PGP Command Line ❶ which key you want to sign by using a unique portion of the UID. (You can sign only with ❷ your own key.) Finally, you enter ❸ your passphrase, and PGP Command Line will sign the other person's key and store it in your keyring.

Updating Keys on a Keyserver

After you sign a key, you can either export the signed public key to a file and return it to the owner, or send the public key with the updated signature back to the keyserver from whence it came. (See Chapter 5 for a full discussion.)

To send the updated key to a keyserver, use the --keyserver-update option.

```
# pgp --keyserver-update UID
```

Now that you know how to manage keys, let's get to the real meat of PGP Command Line: encryption and decryption.

Encryption and Decryption

To encrypt a file with PGP Command Line, use the --encrypt and --recipient flags.

```
# pgp --encrypt filename --recipient UID
```

For example, to encrypt the file BankAccounts.xls when sending it to me (please do!), enter the following:

```
# pgp --encrypt BankAccounts.xls --recipient
mwlucas@blackhelicopters.org
```

This would create an OpenPGP-encrypted file called BankAccounts.xls.pgp.

NOTE *Encrypted files are binary files by default. To encrypt files in ASCII instead, use the --armor flag.*

To decrypt a file, use the --decrypt and --passphrase options:

```
# pgp --decrypt filename --passphrase passphrase
```

For example, to decrypt that same file I would type the following:

```
# pgp --decrypt BankAccounts.xls.pgp --passphrase "This is a
really bad passphrase"
```

Decrypting BankAccounts.xls.pgp creates an unencrypted file called BankAccounts.xls, which I can then open with my office suite.

Signing and Verifying

To sign and verify files, use --sign and --verify. Signed files end in .pgp (.asc if they are in ASCII).

B

GNUPG COMMAND LINE SUMMARY

Throughout this book we've covered various GnuPG commands and options. This appendix collects all the GnuPG functions we've discussed in one quick reference. (It's important to understand the implications of each of these functions, so don't just skip the rest of the book and rely on this appendix.)

GnuPG Configuration

GnuPG stores its configuration information, including keyrings, in a directory. If you're running Windows, you set the location of this directory during the install. On Unix-like systems, that directory defaults to $HOME/.gnupg.

This directory contains three files of concern to most users: gpg.conf, pubring.gpg, and secring.gpg. Your public keyring is in pubring.gpg, and your private keyring is secring.gpg. The gpg.conf file contains all of the GnuPG configuration options.

Output Control

When working with GnuPG keys it's important to decide how the output should be handled. The -a (or --armor) flag tells GnuPG to give output in human-readable format, instead of the default binary format. Similarly, the --output flag tells GnuPG to send its output to a file, rather than dumping it directly to the screen.

Keypair Creation, Revocation, and Exports

To create a new GnuPG keypair, use the interactive --gen-key option. GnuPG will walk you through the key-creation process. (We discussed key creation and management in detail in Chapter 4.)

Revoking a Key

To generate a revocation certificate for your keypair, use the --gen-revoke option, specifying the user ID (UID) of the key you want to revoke. (Using ASCII armor and specifying an output file is optional but probably desirable.)

```
# gpg -a❶ --output mwlucas@blackhelicopters.org.asc.revoke❷
--gen-revoke❸ mwlucas@blackhelicopters.org❹
```

Here we output a file named ❷ mwlucas@blackhelicopters .org.asc.revoke in ❶ ASCII format. This file is a ❸ revocation certificate for the key with a UID that contains the string ❹ mwlucas@blackhelicopters.org. GnuPG will ask you why this key is being revoked and allow you to give a description.

Exporting a Key

To export the key to a text file, use the --export option. (Because this file is plain text, you should use --armor.)

```
# gpg --output pubkey.mwlucas@blackhelicopters.org.gpg.asc❶
--armor❷ --export❸ mwlucas@blackhelicopters.org❹
```

Here we create a file called ❶ pubkey.mwlucas@black-helicopters.org.gpg.asc in ❷ human-readable format, which contains ❸ an export of the key with a UID containing the string ❹ mwlucas@blackhelicopters.org.

Sending a Key to a Keyserver

To send a public key to a keyserver, use the --send-keys option. The --keyserver option lets you choose to which keyserver you want to submit the key. If you don't choose a keyserver, GnuPG will use the default keyserver specified in gpg.conf.

```
# gpg --send-keys❶ mwlucas@blackhelicopters.org❷ --keyserver❸
subkeys.pgp.net❹
```

Here, we ❶ submit a key with the UID containing ❷ mwlu-cas@blackhelicopters.org to ❸ the keyserver ❹ subkeys .pgp.net.

Managing Keyrings

Creating your key will give you your keyring. You'll also need to add keys to and remove keys from this keyring.

Viewing Keys

GnuPG will let you view your keys and various key characteristics:

- To view all the public keys on your keyring, use the option --list-keys. This will print all the keys on your keyring, so you can include a UID or portion thereof to list only particular keys.

- To see the secret keys on your keyring, use the option --list-secret-keys.

- To view the fingerprint of a key, use --fingerprint and the UID of the key or a subset thereof.

Adding and Removing Keys

GnuPG lets you perform all keyserver operations at the command line.

- To receive a key from a keyserver, use the --recv-keys option and the keyid of the key you want to download:

```
# gpg --recv-keys E68C49BC
```

- To import a public key from a file, use the --import option and the name of the file. No other options are required. To remove a key from your keyring, use the --delete-keys option and give the UID or keyid of the key you want to delete.

Key Signatures

Validating, adding, and updating signatures are important parts of GnuPG.

- To view the signatures on a key, use --list-sigs and the keyid or UID.

- To sign a key, use --sign-key and give the keyid or UID:

```
# gpg --sign-key mwlucas@blackhelicopters.org
```

- To export your newly signed public key to a text file, use the --export flag. You probably also want to use --output to place it in a file, and --armor to make it human-readable.

```
# gpg --output gedonner.asc --armor --export
mwlucas@blackhelicopters.org
```

- To upload your signature of this public key to a keyserver, use the --send-keys command and give the keyid or UID of the key you've signed.

- To update the signatures on all the keys in your keyring from a keyserver, use the option --refresh-keys.

- After you sign several keys, use the --update-trustdb option to build your personal Web of Trust.

Encryption and Decryption

Use the --encrypt option to encrypt files, giving the name of the file you want to encrypt as an argument. GnuPG will interactively ask you for the UID of each public key you want to use in the encryption process and then encrypt the files so that they can only be read with the corresponding private key(s).

To decrypt a file, use the --decrypt option. GnuPG will prompt you for your passphrase and print the decrypted message to the terminal.

Signing Files

To sign a file, use the --sign option and give the name of the file you wish to sign. To verify a digital signature, use the --verify option. GnuPG will tell you whether the signature is valid or not.

Output Formats

By default, GnuPG produces encrypted files and keys in binary format and uses filenames based on the original filenames. You can modify this with the --armor and --output options.

- The --armor option tells GnuPG to "armor" its output in human-readable ASCII.

- The --output option lets you choose the name of the file where GnuPG will store its output.

- By default, GnuPG creates a new file with the same name as the original, but with .gpg appended. If you specify --armor, GnuPG creates a new file with the same name but with .asc appended.

Here we encrypt a file in human-readable ASCII and put it in a filename of our own choosing:

```
# gpg --armor --output encryptedfile.asc --encrypt
SecretPasswordList.txt
```

The --armor and --output options must be used before either --sign or --encrypt.

INDEX

Page numbers in italics refer to figures.

Electronic Frontier Foundation
Defending Freedom in the Digital World

Free Speech. Privacy. Innovation. Fair Use. Reverse Engineering. If you care about these rights in the digital world, then you should join the Electronic Frontier Foundation (EFF). EFF was founded in 1990 to protect the rights of users and developers of technology. EFF is the first to identify threats to basic rights online and to advocate on behalf of free expression in the digital age.

The Electronic Frontier Foundation Defends Your Rights!
Become a Member Today!
http://www.eff.org/support/

Current EFF projects include:

Protecting your fundamental right to vote. Widely publicized security flaws in computerized voting machines show that, though filled with potential, this technology is far from perfect. EFF is defending the open discussion of e-voting problems and is coordinating a national litigation strategy addressing issues arising from use of poorly developed and tested computerized voting machines.

Ensuring that you are not traceable through your things. Libraries, schools, the government and private sector businesses are adopting radio frequency identification tags, or RFIDs – a technology capable of pinpointing the physical location of whatever item the tags are embedded in. While this may seem like a convenient way to track items, it's also a convenient way to do something less benign: track people and their activities through their belongings. EFF is working to ensure that embrace of this technology does not erode your right to privacy.

Stopping the FBI from creating surveillance backdoors on the Internet. EFF is part of a coalition opposing the FBI's expansion of the Communications Assistance for Law Enforcement Act (CALEA), which would require that the wiretap capabilities built into the phone system be extended to the Internet, forcing ISPs to build backdoors for law enforcement.

Providing you with a means by which you can contact key decision-makers on cyber-liberties issues. EFF maintains an action center that provides alerts on technology, civil liberties issues and pending legislation to more than 50,000 subscribers. EFF also generates a weekly online newsletter, EFFector, and a blog that provides up-to-the minute information and commentary.

Defending your right to listen to and copy digital music and movies. The entertainment industry has been overzealous in trying to protect its copyrights, often decimating fair use rights in the process. EFF is standing up to the movie and music industries on several fronts.

Check out all of the things we're working on at http://www.eff.org and join today or make a donation to support the fight to defend freedom online.

ELECTRONIC FRONTIER FOUNDATION · 454 SHOTWELL STREET · SAN FRANCISCO, CA 94110 · 415.436.9333

COLOPHON

PGP & GPG was laid out using Adobe InDesign. The font families used are New Baskerville for body text, Futura for headings and tables, and Dogma for titles. The accent color is Pantone 349C.

This book was printed and bound by Lightning Source Incorporated in the U.S.A.

UPDATES

Visit *www.nostarch.com/pgp.htm/* for updates, errata, and other information.

CPSIA information can be obtained at www.ICGtesting.com
Printed in the USA
BVOW06s1101181016

465344BV00001B/1/P